L. RON HUBBARD

THE PHILOSOPHER

THE REDISCOVERY OF THE HUMAN SOUL

CONTENTS

4   AN INTRODUCTION TO L. RON HUBBARD

6   A NOTE ON EXCALIBUR

10   EXCALIBUR
by L. Ron Hubbard

14   THE BIRTH OF DIANETICS

19   THE ORIGINAL THESIS
by L. Ron Hubbard

26   A WORD ON REDISCOVERING
THE HUMAN SOUL

28   THE REDISCOVERY OF THE HUMAN SOUL
by L. Ron Hubbard

36   L. RON HUBBARD DISCUSSES THE
DEVELOPMENT OF HIS PHILOSOPHY

42   SCIENTOLOGY FUNDAMENTALS
by L. Ron Hubbard

52   THE DEMYSTIFICATION OF DEATH

56   THE PHENOMENA OF DEATH
by L. Ron Hubbard

64   DIANETICS, SCIENTOLOGY & BEYOND
by L. Ron Hubbard

68   PHILOSOPHY WINS AFTER 2000 YEARS
by L. Ron Hubbard

74   MY ONLY DEFENSE FOR HAVING LIVED
by L. Ron Hubbard

82   MY PHILOSOPHY
by L. Ron Hubbard

86   EPILOGUE

Photograph by L. Ron Hubbard

ISBN 1-57318-034-3

© 1996 L. Ron Hubbard Library. All Rights Reserved.

Dianetics, Scientology, L. Ron Hubbard Signature, RON Signature, LRH, L. Ron Hubbard, Dianetics Symbol, Scientology Symbol and OT Symbol are trademarks and service marks owned by Religious Technology Center and are used with its permission.

Scientologist is a collective membership mark designating members of the affiliated churches and missions of Scientology. Scientology applied religious philosophy.

Photographs appearing on pages 10, 22, 34-35, 56-57, 58, 60-61 and 63, courtesy of American Stock Photography; photograph appearing on page 37, courtesy of Pacific School of Religion. Item # 3600-58582

The materials of Scientology comprise the largest written and spoken body of any single philosophic work. Those materials have further given rise to the only major religion founded in the twentieth century, and so stand as the spiritual cornerstone for several million adherents across all continents. It was additionally through the philosophy of Scientology that L. Ron Hubbard derived his solutions to criminality, drug addiction, illiteracy and social unrest—all now utilized by many million more in virtually every nation on earth. Yet when we examine the principles upon which that philosophy was founded, we find a truly simple conviction. In the first place, L. Ron Hubbard tells us, wisdom is meant for those who would reach for it, and should never be regarded with awe. Next, he tells us that philosophic knowledge is only relevant to our lives if we can actually apply it, for "learning locked in mildewed books is of little use to anyone." Finally, he tells us that philosophy has no value unless workable or true, and if we come to know the truth about ourselves then the truth shall set us free.

Presented in the pages to follow are ten L. Ron Hubbard articles telling of his philosophic journey to the founding of Dianetics and Scientology. As word of introduction, let us first define philosophy as a love of wisdom or pursuit of wisdom, and say that it traditionally embraces all grand quests for truth. Next, and specifically within that context, let us appreciate the work of L. Ron Hubbard as standing in the oldest philosophic tradition, extending back to at least the dawn of religious thought. Finally, let us describe Scientology as an *applied* religious philosophy and understand it rests, not upon theory or assumption, but upon axioms derived from precise observation. Indeed, when we speak of Ron's philosophic journey, we are actually speaking of the first deliberate and methodical examination of spiritual matters wherein the only criteria had been one of workability, i.e., did procedures derived from that quest actually better our capability to survive, actually make us happier, more causative and more able? In that regard, then, we are not speaking of philosophy in any generally conceived sense: a discourse on existence, a contemplation of reality or a statement of our place in this world. Nor are we speaking of what passes for philosophy in the face of a materialist creed wherein all philosophic thought becomes meaningless beyond such grim platitudes as: *Your life is a biological accident, so you might as well get what you can before you die.* Rather, we are dealing with philosophy as derived from a search for *what is*, for truths that are workable, relevant and applicable to every facet of our lives. Or as Ron himself expressed it, "We are dealing with discoveries."

At the heart of those discoveries lies a truly startling vision of man as an intrinsically spiritual being who lives, not eighty or so years before death makes us nothing, but, in fact, forever. How we might realize that vision is through the process of auditing, which is the central practice of Scientology and defined as the application of Scientology procedures by an auditor, (from the Latin *audire*, to listen). Auditing is a highly precise activity and rests upon the principle that if we can truly grasp the source of what troubles us, then we are no longer troubled. The entirety of Scientology auditing and the training of auditors is delineated by the Scientology Bridge, which, in turn, describes a route to ever greater awareness and ability—whether, as Ron so provocatively phrased it, "the person remains a man or becomes something else."

How L. Ron Hubbard arrived at that statement and what it means within the larger context of our lives is, of course, the primary subject of all that is presented here. As a last introductory word, however, let us emphasize the principal themes. First, those who imagine a remote and contemplative philosopher are about to be disabused; for when we speak of Ron's philosophic journey, we are genuinely speaking of a *journey*—not a sifting of ideas in some academic cloister, but a study of existence from what he truthfully termed "the top down and the bottom up." Next, those who see this subject as largely irrelevant (or at best faintly interesting), are about to be similarly disabused; for here is philosophy, not as a discussion of life, but as a tool for life. In fact, here is philosophy as *life itself*. Finally, and particularly for those already familiar with the works of L. Ron Hubbard, here are various rare essays, selections and discussions from all critical junctures of Ron's philosophic path—from his earliest contemplative work, the now legendary *Excalibur*, through a deeply personal "My Only Defense for Having Lived," to a never previously published conversation with renowned theologian, Dr. Stillson Judah. Additionally included are LRH notes on the phenomena of death, the revelation of past lives and our 1956 title piece, "The Rediscovery of the Human Soul" wherein he recounts a trek through what amounts to the whole of twentieth-century thought to finally arrive at what is a wholly extraordinary philosophic vista:

"We are studying the soul or spirit. We are studying it as itself.

"We are not trying to use this study to enhance some other study or belief. And we are telling the story of how it came about that the soul needed rediscovering."

"We are studying the soul or spirit. We are studying it as itself.
"We are not trying to use this study to enhance some other study or belief."

L. RON HUBBARD

"SUPPOSE ALL THE WISDOM OF THE WORLD *WERE* REDUCED TO JUST ONE LINE—
SUPPOSE THAT ONE LINE WERE TO BE WRITTEN TODAY AND GIVEN TO YOU. ..."

L. RON HUBBARD

Long before the advent of either Dianetics or Scientology, those at all familiar with L. Ron Hubbard had come to expect he would eventually make a remarkable entrance into the philosophic realm. That entrance, largely conceived through the course of an extraordinary week in early 1938, is remembered today as *Excalibur.* In the simplest terms, the work may be described as a first philosophic statement. Previously (and as we shall see in forthcoming articles) he had traveled far and established much as regards a philosophic foundation. Yet here, at the age of twenty-six, came his earliest formal summary, "to align my own ideas," as he modestly termed it, "for my own particular benefit." Given all the manuscript eventually inspired, however—two copies were actually stolen by agents of foreign intelligence services who wished to appropriate those ideas for political ends and only sections remain—such a description seems hardly enough.

At the core of *Excalibur* is Ron's revelatory statement on *survive* as the single common denominator of existence. That all life forms are attempting to survive is, of course, a known datum. But that life is *only* attempting to survive—this was new. Moreover, how he interpreted the datum was new, i.e., a "finite measuring stick," as he elsewhere terms it, with which whole fields of knowledge might be coordinated. Those at all familiar with the works of Herbert Spencer (Ron himself apparently waded through at least the principal ten volumes of *Synthetic Philosophy*) may recognize the concept:

"The proper field and function of philosophy lies in the summation and unification of the results of science. Knowledge of the lowest kind is un-unified knowledge; science is partially unified knowledge; philosophy is completely unified knowledge. Such complete unification requires a broad and universal principle that will include all experience, and will describe the essential features of all knowledge. Is there a feature of this kind?"

To which, of course, *Excalibur* replies unequivocally with *Survive!*

How Ron actually arrived at *survive* is a fairly monumental story, but particularly involves a pivotal sequence of 1937 cytological experiments wherein he was able to demonstrate a cellularly inherited response to toxic substances. That is, having cultured a strain of bacterial cells, the culture was exposed to jets of steam, which affected the cells not at all. Next, applying jets of inherently toxic cigarette smoke, he keenly observed the culture both reacting and retreating from the threat. After continued "taunting" with smoke, he then substituted steam to observe the cells now misidentifying the steam as toxic and similarly retreating. Finally, culturing second and third generations of cells from the first, he found that when these later generation cells were exposed to steam, they likewise misidentified the steam for toxic smoke, and retreated in the name of survival.

If the point seems academic, it is not; for according to Darwinian theory, and hence the foundation of all biological and behavioral thought, learned responses cannot be inherited.

Rather, all life is said to be directed by chance, by a dumb roll of genetic dice as it were. Thus, for example, the ancestral bird develops wings purely as a biochemical function and not according to some inherent thrust towards survival. Yet the moment we introduce survival as a pervasive drive, passed on from cell to cell, we are introducing an *intelligence* behind the scheme of life—an "X-Factor" as Ron initially termed it, that shapes and gives meaning to life in ways that Darwin simply could not explain. As of those first weeks of 1938, and the drafting of his manuscript, Ron would say little more regarding this

X-Factor. But in considering the central message of *Excalibur*, he could not help but wonder who or what first gave that resounding one command, *Survive!*

Needless to say, the scope of *Excalibur* is immense and proposes, not only the means of placing all life—be it human or cellular—into a definitive framework of survive, but a method of resolving any problems related to existence. Or as Ron himself explains, "This book's design is to indicate the true perspective of man's life." That *Excalibur* did not, however, also offer a workable therapy was the principal reason Ron finally chose not to publish the manuscript. That is, if the whole of his quest may be defined in terms of a conviction that philosophy must be workable, must be capable of application, then *Excalibur* could only be regarded as a steppingstone. Nevertheless, with the eventual development of Dianetics, all that is essentially *Excalibur* was made public and, in fact, may be found in *Dianetics: The Modern Science of Mental Health* and *The Dynamics of Life*.

Presented here are the opening pages of *Excalibur*. As an additional word, it might be mentioned that all events recounted here took place in Ron's Port Orchard, Washington, cabin—except, of course, Ron's prefatory note on his near fatal operation at the Bremerton, Washington dental office of Dr. Elbert E. Cone...

Port Orchard, Washington
January 1, 1938

It began with an operation—I took gas as an anesthetic and while under the influence of it my heart must have stopped beating, as in my terror I knew I was slipping through the Curtain and into the land of shades. It was like sliding helter-skelter down into a vortex of scarlet and it was knowing that one was dying and that the process of dying was far from pleasant.

For a long time after I knew that "Death is eight inches below life."

It was terrible work, climbing up out of the cone again, for something did not want to let me back through the wall, and then, when I willed my going, I determined it against all opposition.

And something began to cry out, "Don't let him know!" and then fainter, "Don't let him know."

Though badly shaken I was quite rational when I was restored. The people around me looked frightened—more frightened than I. I was not thinking about what I had been through nearly so much as what I <u>knew</u>. I had not yet fully returned to life. I was still in contact with something. And in that state I remained for some days, all the while puzzling over what I <u>knew</u>. It was clear that if I could but remember I would have the secret of life. This in itself was enough to drive one mad, so illusive was that just-beyond-reach information. And then one morning, just as I awoke, it came to me. I climbed out of my tall ship's bunk and made my way to my typewriter. I began to hammer out that secret and when I had written ten thousand words, then I knew even more clearly. I destroyed the ten thousand and began to write again.

L I B U R

BY L. RON HUBBARD

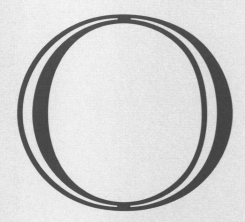nce upon a time, according to a writer in The Arabian Nights, there lived a very wise old man—and wise he must have been— who made it the work of his life to collect all the wisdom in the world.

He wrote an enormous and learned volume, setting forth everything he had found and, at last, sat back contented with a task well done.

Presently, his contentment was dissipated by the thought that he had written too much.

So he sat himself down for ten years more and reduced the original volume to one a tenth its size.

When he had finished, he again thought himself content, but again discovered he was wrong. With painstaking exactitude, he reduced this second work to a single page. Another ten years passed and the ancient philosopher grew even wiser. He took that single page and reduced it to just a single line which contained everything there was to be known.

A decade more found the old scribe close to death.

He had placed that remarkable line in a niche in the wall for safekeeping, intending to tell his son about it.

But now he changed his mind once more.

He tore up even that line.

Suppose all the wisdom of the world *were* reduced to just one line—suppose that one line were to be written today and given to you. With it you could understand the basis of all life and endeavor: love, politics, war, friendship, criminality, insanity, history, business, religion, kings, cats, society, art, mythology, your children, communism, bankers, sailors, tigers, and other matters without end.

More—suppose this one line could tell you all about yourself, could solve all your problems, quiet your restlessness.

If all the wisdom of the world could be compressed into a single line, certainly it would do all these things and more. There *is* one line, conjured up out of a morass of facts and made available as an integrated unit to explain such things. This line is the philosophy of philosophy, thereby carrying the entire subject back into the simple and humble truth.

All life is directed by one command and one command only—SURVIVE!

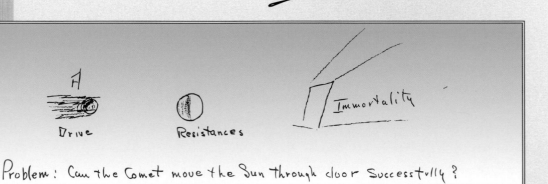

Note and sketch from the Excalibur *manuscript.*

Ron's cabin above Puget Sound, Washington, where Excalibur *was written.*

For five successive years beyond *Excalibur*, Ron continued his examination of *Survive* to effectively determine if more could be derived, extrapolated or discerned. Of special note along this track was his 1940 expedition to North Coast Indian lands off British Columbia, and his examination of mythology as a vehicle for cultural survival, i.e., the myth as a means of perpetuating a tribal identity. He had also grown quite fascinated with those myths apparently rooted in actual events, e.g., the near-universal deluge myth arguably inspired by dim memories from the end of the last Ice Age. Yet in the main, and particularly with the advent of the Second World War, the emphasis lay on practicality. That is, what in the way of a workable therapy could also be drawn from *Survive?*

The answer was, of course, Dianetics, but the route was a tortuous one and finally led through a good deal more: an exhaustive examination of all psychoanalytic theory, an extensive review of then current neural theory, still more cellular study and a series of extraordinary tests on links between hypnosis and insanity. Yet if we are to only retrace the milestones, then our next step lies in the recovery ward of an Oak Knoll Naval Hospital where then Lieutenant L. Ron Hubbard spent the better part of eight months through 1945.

Specifically at issue was the fate of fifteen former prisoners of Japanese internment camps, who, after near-starvation diets through the course of confinement, were found unable to assimilate protein. Even with intensive testosterone treatment, generally effective in thousands of such cases, these unfortunate fifteen essentially continued to starve. In reply, and after extensive scrutiny of the endocrinological link to protein assimilation, LRH proposed a crucial theory: "If the mind regulated the body and not the body regulated the mind," he explained, "then the endocrine system would not respond to hormones if there was in existence a mental block." Whereupon he proceeded with the first formal application of early Dianetics techniques, and so literally saved the lives of those fifteen former prisoners. He also derived a genuinely landmark formulation, i.e., thought took precedence over the physical... Or as he so famously phrased it: "Function monitors structure."

Not generally remarked upon, however, and especially relevant here, are the larger philosophic implications of that statement. For example, with the advent of the first broadly employed antidepressants in the late 1940s, and succeeding generations of psychotropic drugs through the fifties and sixties, the great bulk of what we term mental therapy became a pharmaceutical matter. Specifically, the equation was this: Given all life may be ultimately defined in physiological terms (structure monitors function) then all thought, feeling and emotion is but a consequence of physiology. And should we find those emotions troublesome, then let us alter the chemistry with drugs. Today, of course, the consequence has grown outlandish, with a greater worldwide expenditure on drugs than on food, clothing and shelter combined. But even considering the bottom-line philosophic equation of this chemical worldview, the conclusion is altogether grim. For given the material view of man as a product of chemical recombination through natural selection, then the most we might hope for is the aim of natural selection: a reasonably successful adaptation to our environment... Which, incidentally, remains the great goal of all twentieth-century mental health and a sixty-billion dollar pharmaceutical industry: *Let us become reasonably well adapted before death returns us to a heap of decomposed chemicals.*

Presented here is what followed from that central revelation at Oak Knoll: The first pages of *Dianetics: The Original Thesis* (published today as *The Dynamics of Life*) and, rather ironically, what amounted to a letter of announcement to the American Psychological Association. Regarding the former, let us add that *Original Thesis* contains the earliest formulations on Dianetics, but was largely intended for the professional reader. Although not immediately published, mimeographed copies were circulated among colleagues who, in turn, mimeographed or retyped the manuscript and passed it on to others. In this way, and in remarkably short order, the work engendered a considerable response. Editor-author John W. Campbell Jr., for example, would tell of feverishly retyping from page one to meet a secretary retyping from the final page backwards, all through the course of a single night. Meanwhile, and more to the point, Ron would speak of receiving whole mail bags of requests for additional information.

Inevitably, there were several discussions on how best to bring Dianetics to the world, and just as inevitably consensus was divided. Although Ron had originally envisioned Dianetics as a popular therapy, "for the people and of the people," as he would finally describe his work, neither Campbell nor Michigan physician Dr. Joseph Winter concurred. Rather, and this in the words of Western Electric engineer Donald Rogers, "We tended towards a trickle-down approach," meaning Dianetics would see broadest utilization if first presented to those most logically prepared to appreciate it, i.e., the medical/mental health establishment. If Ron was still not entirely convinced, he nonetheless complied with four letters: one to the American Medical Association, another to the American Psychiatric Association, still another to the Gerontological Society and that which is reprinted here. In concise explanation, he later remarked, "This was the proper thing to do and I did it." While as for the eventual response: "The AMA

simply wrote me, 'Why?' and the APA replied, 'If it amounts to anything I am sure we will hear of it in a couple of years.' "

In fact, they heard of it in thirteen months with the publication of what has become the world's all-time best-selling self-help book, *Dianetics: The Modern Science of Mental Health.* Moreover, and predictably so, both the American Medical Association and American Psychiatric Association would eventually spend considerable time and energy attempting to appropriate Dianetics for economic gain—and, failing that, try and bury it. But in either case, we are looking at an immensely significant philosophic development; for here, and in no uncertain terms, was a philosophy that worked. ▨

"DIANETICS OFFERS THE FIRST ANATOMY OF THE HUMAN MIND AND TECHNIQUES FOR HANDLING THE HITHERTO UNKNOWN REACTIVE MIND, WHICH CAUSES IRRATIONAL AND PSYCHOSOMATIC BEHAVIOR. IT HAS SUCCESSFULLY REMOVED ANY COMPULSIONS, REPRESSIONS, NEUROSES AND PSYCHOSES TO WHICH IT HAS BEEN APPLIED."

L. RON HUBBARD

Box 1796
Savannah, Ga.
April 13, 1949

The American Psychological Assn.
1515 Massachusetts Ave. NW.
Washington, D.C.

Gentlemen;

Working in private research, I have apparently made certain discoveries which I would like to communicate to you for your interest and consideration.

I am accumulating additional data to safeguard this work from undue and unfounded optimism and am preparing a paper for your examination which is entitled: "Certain Discoveries and Researches Leading to the Removal of Early Traumatic Experiences Including Attempted Abortion, Birth Shock and Infant Accidents and Illnesses with an Examination of Their Effects on the Adult Mind and an Account of Techniques Evolved and Employed." .

A very brief résumé of this work follows: In an effort to evolve a better clinical approach to the treatment of certain neuroses and psychoses an intensive study of the early work of Freud was undertaken and revealed certain premises which, for lack of technology, could not be proven in his time. First amongst these was the belief that the unconscious remembered birth. By making certain changes and adaptions in narcosynthesis and combining these with certain techniques of hypnosis but not employing hypnosis as it is currently understood, a trance state was induced in patients and, after considerable practice, they were made to recall the birth experience. It was found in several cases—eight out of the initial series of ten attempted—that the birth experience could be recalled. New traumatic import was discovered and a method was evolved which removed both the force and significance of the trauma. In each case where the experience was reached it was removed with marked and material improvement in the adult life of the patient. In each case treated by this technique even when the birth trauma was not reached but infant traumas were, improvement was definite. In an additional ten cases, with the technique improved, the relieving of the birth trauma was followed by a discovery that prebirth injuries and discomforts could be reached and relieved. In four of these cases abortion had been attempted which was painful to the fetus and the adult psychosis was not improved until the prebirth traumas were relieved. In one case a severe injury to the mother in the sixth month of pregnancy was found to have been recorded by the fetus and to have acted as the underlying cause of a neurosis in the adult. In two cases of prebirth traumas the mother was available and was tested with resultant comparable data of a highly specific nature. In sixteen of the above series of twenty, psychosomatic illnesses were found to have had their chief cause in prebirth or birth traumas. Migraine headache, ulcers, asthma, sinusitis and arthritis were amongst those illnesses relieved.

This letter is not a report of anything but work-in-progress. When an additional twenty cases have been treated, my conclusions will be forwarded to you: at this time I reserve my own professional judgment.

Sincerely,

L. Ron Hubbard

The Original Thesis
by
L. Ron Hubbard

Introduction

n 1932 an investigation was undertaken to determine the dynamic principle of existence in a workable form which might lead to the resolution of some of the problems of mankind. A long research in ancient and modern philosophy culminated, in 1938, in the heuristically discovered primary law. A work was written at that time which embraced man and his activities. In the following years further research was undertaken in order to prove or disprove the axioms so established.

Certain experiences during the war made it necessary for the writer to resolve the work into applicable equations and an intensive program was begun in 1945 toward this end.

A year later many techniques had been discovered or evolved and a nebulous form of the present work was formulated. Financed chiefly by a lump-sum disability compensation, that form of Dianetics was intensively applied to volunteer subjects and the work gradually developed to its present form.

Dianetics has been under test by the writer, as here delineated, for the past four years. The last series of random volunteers, numbering twenty, were rehabilitated, twenty out of twenty, with an average number of work hours of 151.2 per subject. Dianetics offers the first anatomy of the human mind and techniques for handling the hitherto unknown reactive mind, which causes irrational and psychosomatic behavior. It has successfully removed any compulsions, repressions, neuroses and psychoses to which it has been applied.

L. R. H.
January 1948

It was while at Oak Knoll Naval Hospital (above) in 1945 that L. Ron Hubbard began an intensive program to bring his work into applicable equations. In 1950 at his Bay Head, New Jersey residence (inset) he detailed those applicable equations in Dianetics: The Modern Science of Mental Health.

DESCRIPTIC GRAPH OF SURVIVAL

Potential Immortality – Ultimate Pleasure

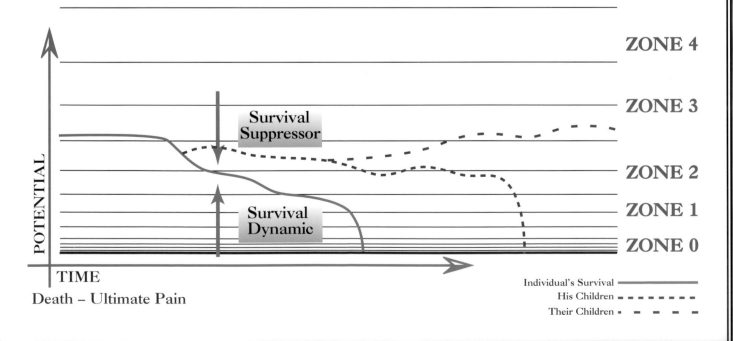

ZONE 4

ZONE 3

Survival
Suppressor

ZONE 2

ZONE 1

Survival
Dynamic

ZONE 0

POTENTIAL

TIME

Death – Ultimate Pain

Individual's Survival ——————
His Children - - - - - -
Their Children - - - - -

Primary Axioms

Dianetics is a heuristic science built upon axioms. Workability rather than idealism has been consulted. The only claim made for these axioms is that by their use certain definite and predictable results can be obtained.

The principal achievement of Dianetics lies in its organization. Almost any of its parts can be found somewhere in history, even when they were independently evolved by the writer. There are no principal sources, and where a practice or a principle is borrowed from some past school the connection is usually accidental and does not admit any further use or validity of that school. Dianetics will work, and can only be worked, when regarded and used as a unity. When diluted by broader applications of older practices, it will no longer produce results. To avoid confusion and prevent semantic difficulties, new and simplified terminology has been used and is used only as defined herein.

Dianetics is actually a family of sciences. It is here addressed in the form of a science of thought applicable to psychosomatic ills and individual aberrations.

The field of thought may be divided into two areas which have been classified as the "knowable" and the "unknowable." We are here concerned only with the "knowable." In the "unknowable" we place that data which we do not need to know in order to solve the problem of improving or curing of aberrations of the human mind. By thus splitting the broad field of thought, we need not now concern ourselves with such indefinites as spiritualism, deism, telepathy, clairvoyance or, for instance, the human soul.

Conceiving this split as a line drawn through the area, we can assign a dynamic principle of existence to all that data remaining in the "knowable" field.

After exhaustive research one word was selected as embracing the finite universe as a dynamic principle of existence. This word can be used as a guide or a measuring stick and by it can be evaluated much information. It is therefore our first and our controlling axiom.

The first axiom is:

Survive!

This can be seen to be the lowest common denominator of the finite universe. It embraces the conservation of energy, all forms of energy. It further delineates the purpose of that energy so far as it is now viewable by us in the "knowable" field. The activity of the finite universe can easily be seen to obey this axiom as though it were a command. All works and energies can be considered to be motivated by it. The various kingdoms have this as their lowest common denominator, for animals, vegetables and minerals are all striving for survival. We do not know to what end we are surviving, and in our field of the "knowable" and in our choice of only the workable axioms, we do not know and have no immediate reason to ask why.

All forms of energy are then surviving to some unknown end, for some unknown purpose. We need only to know that they *are* surviving and that, as units or species, they *must* survive.

By derivation from the first workable axiom, we come into possession of the second. In obedience to the command *survive,* life took on the form of a cell which, joining with other cells, formed a colony. The cell,

GRAPH OF LOGIC
(Simplified for Illustration)

ANSWER

Answer moves from right to left and left to right as wrong or right data are perceived or recalled and evaluated.

WRONG
Survival
Lowered

RIGHT
Potential
Survival
Raised

Each datum weighted for rightness or wrongness. Value of data represented by number of lines wrong to left ⟵, right to right ⟶

The further into the future, the more dynamics can be considered. ↓

Immediate Present

Time

Distant Future

Slightly Wrong Answers ⟵

Slightly Right Answers ⟶

Wrong Answers ⟵

Right Answers ⟶

To ∞ ⟵

To ∞ ⟶

Pain ⟵

Pleasure ⟶

Death ⟵

Immortality ⟶

GRADATION OF WRONGNESS | AREA OF INDECISION | GRADATION OF RIGHTNESS

by procreating, expanded the colony. The colony, by procreating, formed other colonies. Colonies of different types united and necessity, mutation and natural selection brought about specializing which increased the complexity of the colonies until they became an aggregation. The problems of the colonial aggregation were those of food, protection and procreation. In various ways a colonial aggregation of cells became a standardized unity and any advanced colonial aggregation came into possession by necessity, mutation and natural selection, of a central control system.

The purpose of the colonial aggregation was to survive. To do this it had to have food, means of defense, protection and means of procreation. The control center which had developed had as its primary command, *survive!* Its prime purpose was the food, defense, protection and means of procreation.

Thus can be stated the second workable axiom:

The purpose of the mind is to solve problems relating to survival.

The ultimate success of the organism, its species or life would be, at its unimaginable extreme, immortality. The final failure in obedience to the law *survive* would be death. Between eternal survival and death lie innumerable gradations. In the middle ground of such a scale would be mere existence without hope of much success and without fear of failure. Below this point would lie, step by step, innumerable small errors, accidents, losses, each one of which would tend to abbreviate the chances of reaching the ultimate goal. Above this point would lie the small successes, appreciations and triumphs which would tend to secure the desirable goal.

As an axiom, the mind can then be said to act in obedience to a central basic command, *survive,* and to direct or manage the organism in its efforts to accomplish the ultimate goal for the individual or species or life, and to avoid for the individual or species or life any part of the final failure, which leads to the stated axiom:

The mind directs the organism, the species, its symbiotes or life in the effort of survival.

A study of the field of evolution will indicate that survival has been, will be and is the sole test of an organism, whether the organism is treated in the form of a daily activity or the life of the species. No action of the organism will be found to lie without the field of survival, for the organism is acting within its environment upon information received or retained, and error or failure does not alter the fact that its basic impulse was motivated by survival.

Another axiom may then be formulated as follows:

The mind as the central direction system of the body, poses, perceives and resolves problems of survival and directs or fails to direct their execution.

As there are many organisms in the same species, all attempting to accomplish the same end, and as there are many species, and as matter itself is attempting in one unit form or another to survive, there is necessarily conflict and contest amongst the individuals of the species, species or units of matter. Species cannot survive without being interested primarily in the species. Natural selection and other causes have established this as a primary rule for survival: *That the unit remain alive as long as possible as a unit and, by association and procreation, that the species remain alive as a species.* Second-grade interest is paid by the unit or the species to its symbiotes. Third-grade interest is paid to inanimate matter. As this is apparently the most workable solution, natural selection best preserves those species which follow this working rule. And the symbiotes of the successful species therefore have enhanced opportunity for survival.

THE PRIMARY AXIOMS

Survive!

The purpose of the mind is to solve problems relating to survival.

The mind directs the organism, the species, its symbiotes or life in the effort of survival.

The mind as the central direction system of the body, poses, perceives and resolves problems of survival and directs or fails to direct their execution.

The persistency of the individual in life is directly governed by the strength of his basic dynamic.

Intelligence is the ability of an individual, group or race to resolve problems relating to survival.

Man is the most successful organism currently in existence, at least on this planet. Man is currently winning in the perpetual cosmic election which possibly may select the thinker of the new *thought*.

Man is heir to the experience and construction of his own ancestors. As cellular conservatism is one of the factors of survival, his brain is basically the same brain which directed and resolved the problems of his animal forebears. By evolution and natural selection, this brain therefore has the primary priority in emergencies. Superimposed on this animal brain has been developed an enormously complex analyzer, which probably exists in his frontal lobe.

The command, *survive*, is variable in individuals and species to the extent that it may be strong or weak. Superior strength of the command in the individual or species is normally, but variably, a survival factor. The primary facet of personality is the basic strength of the *dynamic* drive.

The *dynamic* is variable from individual to individual and race to race. It is varied by physiology, environment and experience. Its manifestation in the animal brain effects the tenacity of the individual to life or purpose, and it effects the activity of the analyzer. The first characteristic of the individual which should be considered is the basic strength of his *dynamic*. By this an axiom can be formulated:

The persistency of the individual in life is directly governed by the strength of his basic dynamic.

The analytical, human or, as it has elsewhere been called erroneously, the conscious mind, is variable from individual to individual and race to race in its ability to perceive and resolve problems. Another axiom can then be formulated:

Intelligence is the ability of an individual, group or race to resolve problems relating to survival.

It should be noted that there is a distinct difference between the *dynamic* and the intelligence. High intelligence may not denote high *dynamic*. High *dynamic* may not denote high intelligence. *Intelligence* is mental sensitivity and analytical ability. *Dynamic* is the persistency of the individual in obedience to the command, *survive!*

It has been noted that there is a gradation in the scale of survival. Gains toward the ultimate goal are pleasurable. Failures toward the final defeat are sorrowful or painful. Pleasure is therefore the perception of well-being, or an advance toward the ultimate goal. Pain, therefore, is the perception of a reduction toward the final defeat. Both are necessary survival factors.

For the purpose of Dianetics, *good* and *evil* must be defined. Those things which may be classified as *good* by an individual are only those things which aid himself, his family, his group, his race, mankind or life in its dynamic obedience to the command, modified by the observations of the individual, his family, his group, his race or life.

As *evil* may be classified those things which tend to limit the dynamic thrust of the individual, his family, his group, his race or life in general in the dynamic drive, also limited by the observation, the observer and his ability to observe.

Good may be defined as constructive. *Evil* may be defined as destructive—definitions modified by viewpoint. The individual man is an organism attempting to survive in affinity or contest with other men, races and the three kingdoms. His goal is survival for himself, his progeny, his group, his race, his symbiotes, life and the universe in general in contest with any efforts or entities which threaten or impede his efforts to attain the goal.

His happiness depends upon making, consolidating or contemplating gains toward his goal.

It is a purpose of Dianetics to pass man across the abyss of irrational, solely reactive thought and enter him upon a new stage of constructive progression to the ultimate goal.

25

I have been engaged in the investigation of the fundamentals of life, the material universe and human behavior," wrote L. Ron Hubbard of his larger philosophic journey towards Dianetics and Scientology, and proceeded to reference a search "down many highways, through many byroads, into many back alleys of uncertainty." In a further explanation of that search is the introduction and first chapter to a retrospective, "The Rediscovery of the Human Soul."

Begun in 1956, but never completed, the manuscript effectively tells of all that preceded what appears in this publication. As a word of general background, let us add a few salient points: Although events recounted here mark the commencement of Ron's philosophic search, he had previously spent several years, as he elsewhere put it, "poking an inquisitive mind" into related fields. Of special note, were his early psychoanalytic studies with United States Naval Commander Joseph Cheeseman Thompson, who, incidentally, had been the first United States military officer to study under Freud in Vienna, and among the first to enter Freudian theory into the field of ethnology. Also bearing mention was Ron's very early friendship with the deeply spiritual Blackfeet tribesmen in and around his home in Montana, and what amounted to folkloric studies with a locally famous medicine man. The point, in both cases: well before his arrival at George Washington University, Ron had pondered much. Finally, and as referenced here, Ron had also spent nearly two years in a prerevolutionary China and, in fact, had been among the first Westerners after Marco Polo to gain entrance into forbidden Tibetan lamaseries scattered through the southern hills of Manchuria.

Regarding "The Rediscovery of the Human Soul," let us add that in referencing the "fomidable and slightly mad" chief of George Washington University's Psychology Department, he is actually speaking of Dr. Fred August Moss, infamous among students for trick questions and the running of rats through gruesome electrical mazes. Meanwhile the "very famous psychiatrist" who reviews Ron's calculations on human memory capacity was none other than William Alanson White, then superintendent of Washington, DC's St. Elizabeth's Hospital and still celebrated for his outspoken opposition to psychosurgery. Most importantly, however, let us simply understand this: In recalling his work through these years, and particularly his efforts to isolate the repository of human memory, he was factually raising a crucial philosophic question. That is, when we attempt to explain all human memory in terms of purely physical phenomena, we will ultimately find ourselves staring at the singular flaw in the whole of the Western scientific creed. Namely, no diagram of the human brain can account for all we are capable of remembering (much less imagining). It was not for nothing, then, that William Alanson White remarked, in response to Ron's memory calculations, "You have just laid to waste the entire foundation of psychiatric and neurological theory."

Today, of course, psychologists, psychiatrists, neurologists et al., continue to turn themselves inside out in an effort to propose theories broad enough to explain human memory in purely physical terms. (One of the latest involves a model of nonlocalized, or *scattered* memory traces along synaptic contacts so that memories are superimposed upon one another, while another holds that memory is recreated through dynamic neural interplay.) But in either case, questions Ron posed in 1932 are still not answerable within a wholly material context. Hence the increasingly frequent admissions from the scientific community that perhaps, after all, as Ron puts it, "man, as a learned whole, knew damned little about the subject."

"Once upon a time man knew he had a soul; he would have been shocked if he had been told that someday a book would have to be written to inform him, as a scientific discovery, that he had one."

L. RON HUBBARD

OF THE HUMAN SOUL

BY L. RON HUBBARD

INTRODUCTION

nce upon a time man knew he had a soul; he would have been shocked if he had been told that someday a book would have to be written to inform him, as a scientific discovery, that he had one.

And yet that is what this book is about. It is not about *your* soul. It is not designed to tell you to be good or bad or a Christian or a Yogi. It is written to tell you the story of the rediscovery of the human soul as a scientific, demonstrable fact.

Here at a moment when all religions everywhere face extinction by Communism, psychiatry, psychology, dialectic materialism and other "ologies" and "isms" without number, one might believe this book was an effort to create adequate religious fervor to stem the onslaught of the propaganda pamphlets which, all other things aside, are really the most hideous aspect of these threats to man; however this volume seeks no such thing: it is doubtful if religious control of man was very successful either. In the scorch of friction created by such conflicts one might not realize that the soul is worth investigating and writing about for its own sake, not for the sake of capital to be gained from its establishment or extinction.

The tale of the rediscovery of the soul is a considerable adventure entirely from the philosophic and experimental aspect; the adventure has been quite heightened by the amount of preconception and rebuff encountered because of these "isms" and "ologies." One would think that ideologies were quite swollen with their fine opinion of themselves to believe that any investigation of the soul would of course be meant as a personal affront to each or all.

One conceives the view, after he has been awhile investigating the soul, that amongst all these modern disagreements there existed only one agreement: that the subject of the human soul, for bad or good, was only within the personal sphere of each. Thus, publishing this book will in itself be an adventure for it will discover amongst these "isms" and "ologies," each one, the conceit that it itself is being attacked, and to "attack" that many oppositions at one fell charge requires in an author either the hide of a rhinoceros, the Citadel of a Christophe, or the legs of an impala. Having none of these but only a certain confidence in the stupidity of all these schools of slavery we locate in ourselves a willingness to accept the risk if not the combat.

Our main controversy, quite aside from minor ones, is whether or not the soul or knowledge about it could be considered a "scientific subject." For by definition in these dialectic times, science is a somethingness which considers itself concerned entirely with matters of matter and has sought to accumulate to itself alone—much like other "isms" and "ologies"—the entire proprietorship of knowledge and has then sought to demonstrate that knowledge is only to be found in materialism. This somewhat detoured view becomes artificial on its first inspection. "Science" means only "truth" being derived from the Latin word "scio" which is "knowing in the fullest sense of the word"; more severely and lately used, "science" infers an organization of knowledge: and if this is the case, then this material concerning the human soul, being based on critically observational knowledge and being organized, certainly meets the criteria of "scientific" knowledge.

Being then, based on observable, mensurable truth or knowledge and being organized, we assigned to this body of information about the human soul, the word *Scientology,* which is to say, the "knowledge of knowledge" or "knowing how to know" or "study of truth," thus and thereby, with the word, taking sides with the "ologies." But we could just as well call this material "soulism" or "the doctrine of the human soul" and take the alignments of the "isms," thus, so to speak, edging over on the good side of each and thus avoiding war.

Scientology as a word is quite necessary since we need an identifying symbol to represent these particular discoveries and data and the methodology of their use and to prevent our making errors in conversation; the subject of the soul lends itself readily to any branch of any knowledge, and to keep oriented and localized with the information contained herein we need the word.

Very well, now that we have, we hope, announced our political climate—or lack of one—and have given a word to what we are doing, let us examine WHAT we are doing.

We are studying the soul or spirit. We are studying it as itself. We are not trying to use this study to enhance some other study or belief. And we are telling the story of how it came about that the soul needed rediscovering. And now that we've rediscovered it, we are also discovering if the information thus attained can in any way assist us to live better, or for that matter, die better.

Thus you can plainly see that this book is perfectly safe to read. It does not seek to alter your ideological or religious beliefs. If these alter simply because you read this book, no one is to blame but yourself and it was not the author's intention to tamper.

Of course if you DO read this book and do its few simple experiments, your ideological and religious beliefs will alter, there's no doubt of that. However, remember, should the idea of blaming anyone occur to you, that whatever actually HAPPENS, we didn't really INTEND to change your philosophic pattern—all we intended to do, quite innocently, was to give you some data about the human soul—not even your own soul, just the soul in general.

The story starts in the physics laboratories of George Washington University in 1930. Quite coincidentally at almost this same time Professor Thomas Brown in charge of that department, was launching experiments which within fifteen years would bring forth an atomic bomb upon earth largely through Dr. George Gamow an assistant in this same laboratory.

Unwitting of the ferocity being planned within a few yards of me, I was engaged upon an experiment about poetry. Now usually poetry has little to do with a physics lab but this time it did. Majoring in engineering a trifle under duress and studying nuclear physics with a skeptical eye, my tedium had found a relief in conceiving that one might find why poetry in any language sounded like poetry whether one spoke the language or not.

Using an aged Koenig photometer to measure voice vibrations I was reading a line of Browning and then a line of prose alternately and studying any difference between the symmetry of vibrations in the poetry as contrasted to the prose. I discovered after a little, that there was a definite symmetry and was about to concoct a more complex test when it struck me that the mind was NOT a Koenig photometer. I drew back and looked studiously at the ugly machine with its four mirrors and glass frame and commented to myself that it would be a frighteningly uncomfortable thing to have kicking about between one's ears. BUT if one did not have one between one's ears, one DID or at least MUST have some kind of mechanism which would translate and measure not only the impulse of sound but also the symmetry of that sound. And, having measured it, that something did the additional trick not only of storing that symmetry but of recalling and viewing it at will.

Thus was born a search, a search which went on for a quarter of a century. Thus was born the train of intuition, observation and experiment which finally rediscovered, as a scientific fact, the soul, and gained methods of doing things to it, for it and with it with scientific certainty.

But here in 1930, serving out my time in "the salt mines of F Street" no such serious end was in real view. My interest, I must confess, went more to soaring planes at Congressional Airport, upsetting the faculty by my articles in the university paper and always making sure that the most demanded girl on the campus was the sweetheart of the professional engineering fraternity and mine to dance with, of course.

Probably nothing would have come of my search at all if I had not tried to solve something of the problem by calling on the formidable and slightly mad chief of the psychology department. He, in the secrecy of his opinions of his fellows, mainly wanted to know what I was doing out of the Engineering School and why I didn't leave such

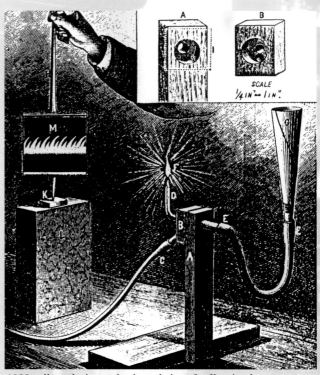

1928 college physics textbook rendering of a Koenig photometer.

things properly to psychologists. This challenged me a trifle. As a sensitive youth, soiled by the courtesy of the Orient in which I had spent much precollege time, I objected to people being so thoroughly Occidental, and after I had laughed at him a few columns in the university paper, I wheedled all the psychology textbooks out of a psychology major whose themes in English class I used to write and heavied my eyelids but not my understanding by studying them hard during my German and surveying lectures which bored me intensely anyway. But though I studied and comprehended what I read, the comprehension I began to believe was a trifle one-sided. These texts, like the courtesy of the psychology dean, were somewhat wanting.

Like the picture of the picture of the picture on the cereal box, psychology simply assigned all this first to the brain and then to the cell. Going no further, it still failed to describe any sound-recording-recalling devices. With youthful scorn I consigned psychology to that moldy heap of pretenses which so often pass their polysyllabic nonsense off as learning and decided to think some more about thinking—a trick to say the least.

About this time a biology major and I were accustomed to meeting after classes at (bygone days) a speak-easy up 21st Street for a round of blackjack and a couple shots after classes and whilst trying to detour my eyes from his nimble fingers he regaled me with bits and things about what went on in the world of biology. One day he actually did manage to slip me the card I didn't want by

remarking to me that the brain contained an exorbitant number of molecules of protein and that each molecule "had been discovered" to have holes in it. Fascinated, I bled him of data and a few days later made the time to calculate memory.

It seemed to me that if molecules had holes in them to a certain number, then memory, perchance, might be stored in these holes in the molecules. At least it was more reasonable than the texts I had read. But the calculation, done with considerably higher math than psychologists or biologists use, yet yielded a blank result. I calculated that memory was "made" at a certain rate and was stored in the holes in these punched protein molecules in the form of the most minute energy of which we had any record in physics. But despite the enormous number of molecular holes and the adequate amount of memory, the entire project yielded only this result: I was forced to conclude, no matter how liberal I became, that even with this system, certainly below cellular level, the brain did not have enough storage for more than three months of memory. And in that I could recall things quite vividly, at least before the beginning of the semester, I was persuaded that either the mind could not remember anything or that much smaller energy particles existed than we knew about in nuclear physics.

Amusing, a decade later, this theory, which I had imparted to a very famous psychiatrist complete with the figures, came back as an Austrian "discovery" and was widely accepted as the truth. I always wondered at the psychiatrist's carelessness in losing that last page which declared by the same calculations that the mind could not remember.

Laying it all aside for a long time I was yet recalled to my calculations by physics itself. There are some odd movements noticeable in atomic and molecular phenomena which aren't entirely accounted for and supposing that a "smaller" energy might make these movements amongst the larger particles, I came face to face with the grossness of the measuring equipment with which we have always worked in physics. We have only streams of electrons even today to "see small." And I was so struck with the enormity of the Terra Incognita which physics had yet to invade that it seemed far simpler to do what I eventually did—went off and became a science fiction writer.

Living the rather romantic life of an author in New York, Hollywood and the Northwest, going abroad into savage cultures on expeditions to relax, I did little about my search until 1938 when a rather horrible experience took my mind closer to home than was my usual mental circuit. During an operation I died under the anesthetic.

Brought back to unwillingly lived life by a fast shot of adrenalin into the heart, I rather frightened my rescuers by sitting up and saying, "I know something if I could just think of it."

In my woods cabin in the Northwest I had quite a little while to think of it. The experience had made me ill enough to keep me in a reading frame of mind and I didn't get far from a teapot, a blanket and books for some weeks.

The alarm caused those "nearest to me" when I sought to regale them with this adventure of death, amused me. That they were not disturbed that I had actually and utterly died medically and coroneresquely, they were dismayed that I would talk about it. Deciding it was not a popular subject I nevertheless looked into the rather extensive library I sported and found that the thing was not unknown in human experience and that a chap named Pelley had even founded a considerable religious study on it. Quite plausibly he went to heaven and came back and lived to tell of it.

The psychiatric texts which I kept around for unpronounceable ailments to put in the mouths of my fictional doctors were as thoroughly alarmed as my near of kin. They called any such experiences by a nice ugly name, "delusion" and made fat paragraphs out of its mental unhealthiness. Only in that matter of unhealthiness could I agree with them. I always have, always will and did then consider that dying was unhealthy. They also seemed to feel that people who died ought to stay dead. Concluding that the littleness they knew about such happenings was best expressed by the voluminous inconclusions they wrote about it, I turned to the classic philosophers and while these had much to say, very little of it was concisely to the point.

I realized, after wandering through some five hundred pounds of texts, some things which altered my life quite a bit more than merely dying. During those weeks in the cabin my studies pressed me toward some conclusions. I concluded first that dying had not been very damaging. I concluded second that man, as a learned whole, knew damned little about the subject. For better or worse, I concluded that man had better know not just a little more about dying but a lot more about man.

And that shaped my destiny.

I n November, 1958, at the request of Doctor Stillson Judah, Professor of Religious History, Ron discussed both the philosophic background and working principles of Dianetics and Scientology. Although some of what is talked of here—Ron's examination of poetry, for example— has been touched upon earlier, the perspective is unique; for with Dr. Stillson Judah we have a man much intrigued with ideas, and it is the grand progression of L. Ron Hubbard's thinking he seeks through the course of this conversation.

Also keenly relevant here are Ron's statements on what followed from work at Oak Knoll, including the publication of *Dianetics: The Modern Science of Mental Health* and, thereafter, his recognition of "what was looking at the pictures." As a point of interest on the latter, his entrance into the spiritual realm actually followed from research in Wichita, Kansas and irrefutable evidence that we do not live only once.

L. RON HUBBARD DISCUSSES THE DEVELOPMENT OF HIS PHILOSOPHY

Dr. Judah:

Where did the subject of Dianetics and Scientology start?

LRH:

The whole subject was born out of engineering. Both of these subjects extend from engineering, which was taken on top of my study in the Orient as a boy. From the age of about sixteen, to

Dr. Stillson Judah

about twenty-one, I spent a great deal of my time in the Orient and I was well acquainted with various Oriental schools. I came back and my father forced me to take physical science as a religion, which gave me a background of mathematics and physics. My basic interest was the field of religion—Buddhism, Taoism were fascinating to me. However, I didn't think they were very good for people, or they couldn't possibly contain all the answers, for this one reason: the people who were practicing them were poor,

L. Ron Hubbard in his 19th Street Washington, DC office where he was interviewed by Dr. Stillson Judah.

unhealthy and in very bad relationship to the physical universe.

So quite by accident, in 1932, I was working down here in a George Washington University laboratory, and I was trying to add up poetry. I couldn't understand why poetry read in Japanese would obviously be poetry to somebody who spoke only English—why poetry of various kinds was poetry, even when translated. What was this thing about poetry?

I went over and picked up a Koenig photometer, one of these little gas photometers, that you talk against the diaphragm, and it gives you vocal vibrations. I made graphs of poetry and I wanted to know how the mind responded to those sounds—why the mind responded to those sounds. I could not get any real basis for why did the mind respond to certain sounds and rhythms and not to others? Why did the mind differentiate between noise and a note, for instance? And this didn't seem to me to be a covered subject in my field. And I became interested enough to go up to George Washington University's psychology laboratory, at that time run by Dr. Fred August Moss, and he floored me—I hadn't known something; I hadn't known we didn't know.

> **"In 1938, I decided totally that nobody had stated, neither Darwin nor in the field of evolution, the basic principle of existence."**
>
> L. RON HUBBARD

It was a very odd thing, for anybody to be educated in the engineering sciences—where you know what you know when you know it and how you know it—to be given a bunch of statements which didn't explain at all my problem. I was simply an engineer taking on confidence the fact that all other sciences, even those in human relations, were all understood, and I ran into somebody who could not answer my questions. And I read all of the books I could find, down here in the Library of Congress, on psychology and the mind. I found out I was looking at a field that didn't know what it knew. It was a baffling thing to me. I turned around to philosophies of various kinds. I made this a very positive hunt and it wasn't until 1938 that I was totally convinced we didn't know.

We didn't have a basic principle of existence. There was no point of jump-off for the human mind, or the study of the human spirit. We didn't even know what a spirit was. We didn't have a definition for it. We said where it went, and what would happen to it, and how it could be punished, but we never said what it was, what was its relationship?

These questions could have been answered perhaps in some field, somewhere, at some time, but I just couldn't seem to find the answers. Whether it was Nietzsche or Schopenhauer, Kant, or any of the rest of them. These men were all groping. So I said, here's a wide-open field.

I have the world's worst grades in the university because I was interested in everything except my subject. Between my leaving the university and 1938, we were in a depression. Any job that I had had offered me was long gone by the time I stepped out. And I used my engineering in the field of writing science fiction—I made very well at it. I spent a whole career before World War II as a successful writer. I was in Hollywood, went on three expeditions to study wild and savage peoples and find out what they thought about things, and I paid for them with writing. And I did very well as a writer, I was president of the American Fiction Guild and so on. But all this time, all I was really doing was trying to eat, and pay my way, and pay for my research, and finally get up to some point where I had some clue.

In 1938, I decided totally that nobody had stated, neither Darwin nor in the field of evolution, the basic principle of existence. And I said then, for good or bad, I'm going to have to state one, in order to launch any sort of a further investigation, because all I had done was look at question marks. And I did.

The basic work that I wrote has never been published. I wrote a 125,000-word work, and it has never seen the light of day.

Dr. Judah:

Why was that?

LRH:

It was an attempt to organize knowledge on the basis of a dynamic principle of existence to see if it could be done; if it gave us answers in the field of the spirit. I didn't think of improving anybody or explaining religion.

It did bring me to an understanding, on an evaluation basis, of the dynamic principle of existence:

to survive, or survival. I tried to evaluate along this line, very heavily, to see where we got, because the one common denominator I could find in all races, types and activities, was survival. Everybody seemed to be trying for survival. And when they no longer tried for survival, then they tried for its opposite, succumb. And these two things seemed to go together as the motivating principles of life.

War came along and because I knew Asia I was thrown into Naval Intelligence, and during the remainder of the war, when we lost in the Far Pacific early in the war, they returned nearly everybody who had been involved in it home and they wouldn't send them out there anymore. So they gave me command of a corvette, and I finished up the war as a line officer.

But tremendously interesting things occurred, during this period—tremendous subjects for study, all this time. I had one crew that was a hundred percent criminals. They were all criminals. They had just taken them right straight out of Portsmouth, and issued them with this corvette. A hundred men. And I spent the last year of my naval career in a naval hospital. Not very ill, but I had a couple of holes in me—they wouldn't heal. So they just kept me.

Everywhere I looked, I seemed to find men who were in difficulty—men who couldn't rationalize why they were there, they didn't know what they were doing, and I said maybe the answer lies in the glandular system, maybe this is the material answer after all. I spent most of that year down in the medical library studying the endocrine system, trying to find out if it got anywhere—and every answer led back to the fact that man was motivated by something I had not yet put my finger on.

To make a long story short, after the war I returned to writing, but mostly to Dianetics and its preparation. And I found out what was entangling man—he was tangling himself up with combinations of mental image pictures. And if you could do something to the pictures you could do something to the man. Quite interesting. And I entered now in a safe sound field, where I was concerned. We were in a sound field of engineering. There was an energy, you could measure these pictures, they weren't imaginary. I found out they were measurable, and did measure them. You had your hands on some mass, and you could produce a positive effect, and things were traceable.

I was persuaded by Hermitage House to write a popular book on the subject. And that book, *Dianetics: The Modern Science of Mental Health*, brought me a lot of embarrassment. And the embarrassment was this: I had no organization, I had no finance, I had nothing, and all of a sudden the world was pounding on my door.

> "I FOUND THAT YOU COULD IMPROVE THE GOODNESS OF A MAN BY IMPROVING THE MAN, AND HE WAS MORE OR LESS BASICALLY GOOD."
>
> L. RON HUBBARD

Dr. Judah:

This was the new mousetrap.

LRH:

Always the new mousetrap, that's for sure. College students came from every part of this country, people from all over the world. And I found they presented cases I had never seen before. They presented greater difficulties than I had seen. And I didn't know what to do with many of these people—I knew my study was a long way from end. I wanted to get the answers to this, and get this story written just a little further.

In the fall of 1951, I found out what was looking at the pictures. Here we had mental image pictures, and up to that time I had been studying them and their behavior, which is the reaction, stimulus-response mechanisms that psychology itself had been familiar with, but never had analyzed. I found out what was looking at the pictures. And described it. And found out that you could do things with it from a very practical standpoint that nobody had ever done before, and found myself suddenly in the field of religion, whether I wanted to be or not, there I was. Very simple—the human soul was the fellow.

This rather upset things, because most religions speak to men about "you've got to take care of *your* soul." This wasn't the case according to my findings. The fellow I was talking to was the soul.

I knew how many years a Buddhist can sit and meditate, and how long a Lama priest can work, in order to get a detached view of things. And I found out that on a great many people, some 50 percent of the people I ran into, I could attain this detached view of things in a matter of minutes. So I knew I wasn't looking at a weird phenomenon, or a psychotic manifestation. I found out that psychiatry had known something about this but they merely said that was a sure sign of craziness. But man was his own spirit. And whether I liked it or not, I was in the middle of a religion.

Dr. Judah:

What happened after this?

LRH:

I went on from there working to find out what was the behavior of this thing called the human spirit. And I felt to some degree I had arrived. At first I didn't even know that it wasn't a mass factor. And don't think I didn't have to turn my self around and upside down, because I had pretty well accustomed myself to thinking in totally scientific, totally realistic lines. And when I was dealing with something I couldn't sense, measure or experience but which was there, I certainly was going to sense, measure and experience and know the reason why. And I did, over in London, in 1953, I built a meter which measures the responses of this thing while exteriorized from a being, this thing.

I finally got myself satisfied as to the fact that I was really looking at the thing that looked at the pictures—the thing that experienced the pictures; the thing that motivated the pictures—and realized that unless you improved a man spiritually, in a most engineering sense all we could do was change his habit patterns. I found that you could improve the goodness of a man by improving the man, and he was more or less basically good. This was a very great stroke of luck, as far as I was concerned. When you freed a man and separated him from past punishment, you found that he was good. That was a rather fabulous thing. Therefore we find ourselves in the middle of a moral and ethical science, which applies to nothing more nor less than the human spirit. ▨

The materials of Dianetics and Scientology are contained in more than 5,000 writings and 3,000 tape-recorded lectures. In the main, those materials are concerned with the *application* of LRH philosophic principles—the auditing processes towards greater awareness and ability, the assist processes for the relief of physical illness and emotional distress, the means for resolving difficulties in the workplace, ethical failings, learning disabilities and, frankly, much, much more. Yet the philosophic root of Dianetics and Scientology, the core truth upon which all is based, could hardly be simpler: "The spirit is the source of all," Ron tells us, "You are a spirit."

It is a unique statement, and factually found nowhere else in the whole of philosophic, religious or scientific thought. For example, although Ron himself describes Scientology as a very basic psychology, he is speaking of psychology in its original sense, i.e., the "study of the spirit." In practice, however, the psychologist has denied the spirit utterly. While even in somewhat more comparative Eastern religions, one finds nothing as exalted as L. Ron Hubbard's statement on our spiritual essence.

In what amounts to a comprehensive explanation of that statement, Ron presents "Scientology Fundamentals." It dates from 1956, was originally described as "the results of fifty thousand years of thinking men," and was intended as the definitive introduction to a philosophy, as Ron so descriptively phrased it, dedicated to "the freeing of the soul by wisdom."

AUDITING SESSION

AUDITOR

MENTAL IMAGE PICTURES

IN AN AUDITING SESSION THE AUDITOR HELPS ANOTHER PERSON LOCATE AND EXAMINE HIDDEN SOURCES OF DIFFICULTIES, INCLUDING MENTAL IMAGE PICTURES CONTAINING PHYSICAL PAIN, TRAUMA AND PAINFUL EMOTIONS. AUDITING, THEN, IS THE MEANS BY WHICH ONE CAN BECOME MORE AWARE OF WHO HE IS, WHAT HAS HAPPENED TO HIM AND THE EXTENT OF HIS TRUE POTENTIAL.

SCIENTOLOGY FUNDAMENTALS

BY L. RON HUBBARD

What is Scientology?

Scientology is an applied religious philosophy.

The term *Scientology* is taken from the Latin word *scio* (knowing in the fullest sense of the word) and the Greek word *logos* (study of). In itself the word means literally *knowing how to know*.

Scientology is further defined as the study and handling of the spirit in relationship to itself, universes and other life.

Any comparison between Scientology and the subject known as psychology is nonsense. Early psychology such as that begun by St. Thomas Aquinas and extended by many later authors was, in 1879, interrupted severely by one Professor Wundt, a Marxist at Leipzig University in Germany. This man conceived that man was an animal without soul and based all of his work on the principle that there was no *psyche* (a Greek word meaning spirit). Psychology, the study of the spirit (or mind) then came into the peculiar position of being "a study of the spirit which denied the spirit." For the subsequent decades, Wundtian "psychology" was taught broadly throughout the world. It taught that man was an animal. It taught that man could not be bettered. It taught that intelligence never changed. This subject, Wundtian psychology, became standard, mainly because of the indifference or lack of knowledge of people in charge of universities.

Scientology can and does change behavior and intelligence, and it can and does assist people to study life. Unlike Wundtian pseudopsychology, it has no political aspiration. Scientology is not teaching dialectical materialism under the heading of "psychology."

Scientology is a *route*, a way, rather than a dissertation or an assertive body of knowledge.

Through its drills and studies one may find the truth for oneself. It is the only thing that can show you who *you* really are.

The technology is therefore not expounded as something to believe but something to *do*.

The end result of Scientology studies and drills is a renewed awareness of self as a spiritual and immortal being.

Only those who believe, as do psychiatrists and psychologists, that man is a soulless animal or who wish for their own reasons to keep man unhappy and oppressed are in any conflict with Scientology.

Scientology, used by the trained and untrained person, improves the health, intelligence, ability, behavior, skill and appearance of people.

It is a precise and exact science, designed for an age of exact sciences.

It is employed by an *auditor* upon individuals or small or large groups of people in their presence. The auditor makes these people, at their choice, do various exercises, and these exercises bring about changes for the better in intelligence, behavior and general competence.

ATTENTION

Scientology is employed as well by business and government persons to solve problems and to establish better organization.

It is also employed by the average person to bring better order into life.

HOW IS SCIENTOLOGY USED?

Scientology is employed by an auditor as a set of drills upon the individual, and small or large groups. It is also employed as an educational subject. It has been found that persons can be processed in Scientology with Scientology exercises and can be freed from their major anxieties and can become brighter, more alert and more competent. *But* if they are *only* processed they have a tendency to be overwhelmed or startled, and although they may be brighter and more competent they are still held down by an ignorance of life. Therefore it is far better to teach *and* process a person than only to process him. In other words, the best use of Scientology is through processing and education in Scientology. In this way there is no imbalance. It is interesting that people only need to study Scientology to have some small rise in their own intelligence, behavior and competence. The study itself is therapeutic by actual testing.

It is also used by business and government leaders to establish or improve organization.

It is used as well by the individual at home or at his work to make a better life.

IS SCIENTOLOGY VALID?

Tens of thousands of case histories, all sworn to, are in the possession of the organizations of Scientology. No other subjects on Earth except physics and chemistry have had such grueling testing. Scientology in the hands of an expert can restore man's ability to handle any and all of his problems. Scientology is used by some of the largest companies on Earth. It is valid. It has been tested. It is the only thoroughly tested system of improving human relations, intelligence and character, and is the only one which does.

BASIC PRINCIPLES

Like engineering, Scientology has certain basic principles. These are necessary to a full understanding of the subject. It is not enough to know how to process people in Scientology. To be effective one must also know the basic principles. Scientology is very exact. The humanities of the past were full of opinions. Scientology is full of facts that work.

To study Scientology one should scan quickly through the basics and find something with which one can agree. Having found *one thing* with which he can agree, one should then skim through again and find another fact. One should continue to do this until he feels some friendliness to the subject. When one has achieved this, and *only* when one has achieved this, he should then study all the basic principles. There is no effort here to be authoritarian. No one will try to make the subject difficult.

You may have been taught that the mind is a very difficult thing to know about. This is the first principle of Scientology: It is possible to know about the mind, the spirit and life.

THE PARTS OF MAN

The individual man is divisible into three parts.

The first of these is the spirit, called in Scientology the *Thetan*.

The second of these parts is the *Mind*.

The third of these parts is the *Body*.

Probably the greatest discovery of Scientology and its most forceful contribution to the knowledge of mankind has been the isolation, description and handling of the human spirit, accomplished in July 1952 in Phoenix, Arizona. I established along scientific rather than religious or humanitarian lines that that thing which is the person, the personality, is separable from the body and the mind at will and without causing bodily death or mental derangement.

In ages past there has been considerable controversy concerning the human spirit or soul, and various attempts to control man have been effective in view of his almost complete ignorance of his own identity. Latterly, spiritualists isolated from the person what they called the astral body, and with this they were able to work for various purposes of their own. In Scientology, the spirit itself was separated from what the spiritualists called the astral body and there should be no confusion between these two things. As you know that you are where you are at this moment, so you would know if you, a spirit, were detached from your mind and body. Man had not discovered this before because, lacking the technologies of Scientology, he had very little reality upon his detachment from his mind and body; therefore, he conceived himself to be at least in part a mind and a body. The entire cult of communism is based upon the fact that one lives only one life, that there is no hereafter and that the individual has no religious

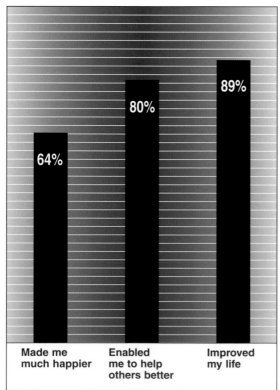

What People Say Scientology Has Done For Them

Made me much happier	Enabled me to help others better	Improved my life
64%	80%	89%

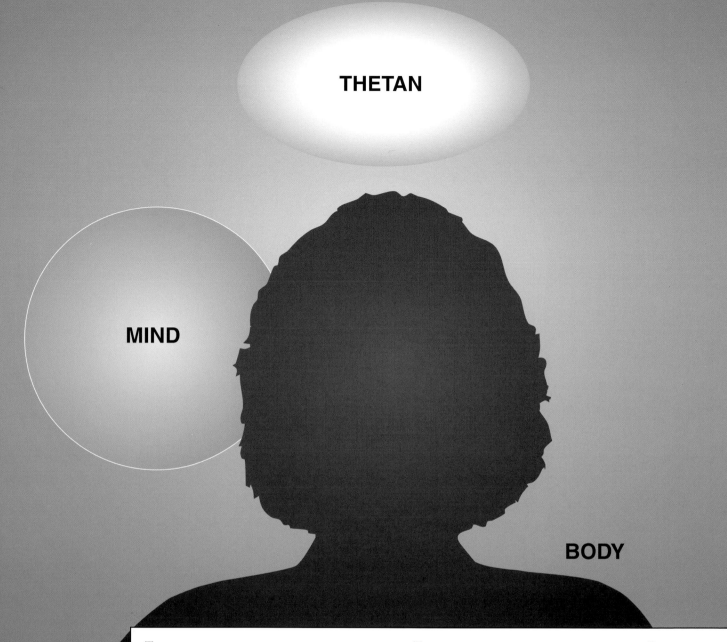

THE INDIVIDUAL MAN IS DIVISIBLE INTO THREE PARTS. THE FIRST OF THESE IS THE SPIRIT, CALLED IN SCIENTOLOGY, THE THETAN. THE SECOND OF THESE PARTS IS THE MIND. THE THIRD OF THESE PARTS IS THE BODY.

significance. Man at large has been close to this state for at least the last century. The state is of a very low order, excluding as it does all self-recognition.

THE SPIRIT

The thetan is described in Scientology as having no mass, no wavelength, no energy and no time or location in space except by consideration or postulate. The spirit, then, is not a *thing*. It is the *creator* of things.

The usual residence of the thetan is in the skull or near the body. A thetan can be in one of four conditions. The first would be entirely separate from a body or bodies, or even from this universe. The second would be near a body and knowingly controlling the body. The third would be in the body (the skull) and the fourth would be an inverted condition whereby he is compulsively away from the body and

cannot approach it. There are degrees of each one of these four states. The most optimum of these conditions, from the standpoint of man, is the second.

A thetan is subject to deterioration. This is at first difficult to understand since the entirety of his activity consists of considering or postulating. He uses, through his postulates, various methods of controlling a body. That he does deteriorate is manifest, but that he can at any moment return to an entirety of his ability is also factual. In that he associates beingness with mass and action, he does not consider himself as having an individual identity or name unless he is connected with one or more of the games of life.

The processes of Scientology can establish this for the individual with greater or lesser rapidity, and one of the many goals of processing in Scientology is to "exteriorize" the individual and place him in the second condition

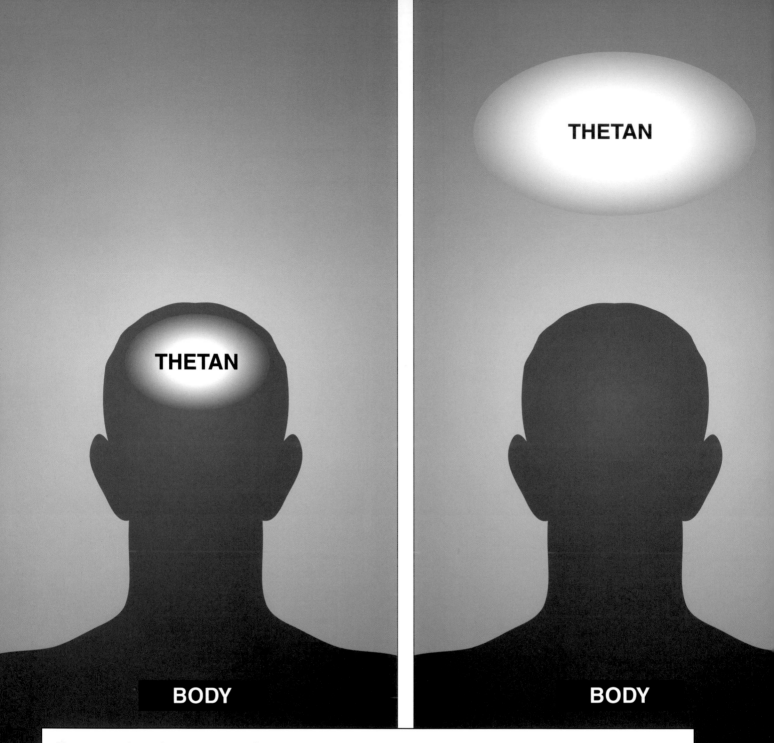

THE THETAN (SPIRIT) IS DESCRIBED IN SCIENTOLOGY AS HAVING NO MASS, NO WAVELENGTH, NO ENERGY AND NO TIME OR LOCATION IN SPACE. THE SPIRIT THEN IS NOT A THING. IT IS THE CREATOR OF THINGS. THE USUAL RESIDENCE OF THE THETAN IS IN THE SKULL OR NEAR THE BODY.

above, since it has been discovered that he is happier and more capable when so situated.

THE MIND

The *mind* is a communication and control system between the thetan and his environment. The mind is a network of communications and pictures, energies and masses, which are brought into being by the activities of the thetan versus the physical universe or other thetans. A thetan establishes various systems of control so that he can continue to operate a body and through the body operate things in the physical universe, as well as other bodies. The most obvious portion of the mind is recognizable by anyone not in serious condition. This is the "mental image picture." In Scientology we call this mental image picture a *facsimile* when it is a "photograph" of the physical universe sometime in the past. We call this mental image picture a *mock-up* when it is created by the thetan or for the thetan and does not consist of a photograph of the physical universe. We call a mental image picture a *hallucination* or, more properly, an *automaticity* when it is created by another and seen by self.

Various phenomena connect themselves with this entity

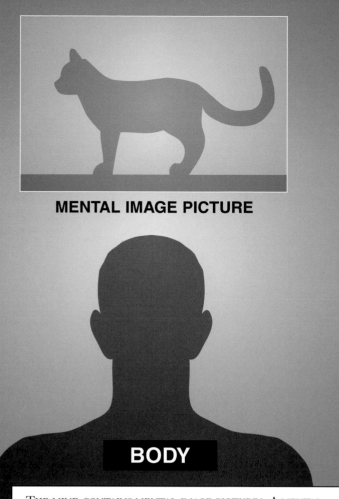

MENTAL IMAGE PICTURE

BODY

THE MIND CONTAINS MENTAL IMAGE PICTURES. A MENTAL IMAGE PICTURE IS CALLED A "FACSIMILE" WHEN IT IS A "PHOTOGRAPH" OF THE PHYSICAL UNIVERSE. IT IS CALLED A "MOCK-UP" WHEN IT IS CREATED BY THE THETAN AND IS NOT A "PHOTOGRAPH" OF THE PHYSICAL UNIVERSE.

called the mind. Some people closing their eyes see only blackness, some people see pictures. Some people see pictures made by body reactions. Some people see only black screens. Others see golden lines. Others see spaces, but the keynote of the entirety of the system called the mind is postulate and perception. Easily ten thousand new, separate mental phenomena, not hitherto seen by earlier observers, have been classified in Scientology and Dianetics.

The thetan receives, by the communication system called the mind, various impressions, including direct views of the physical universe. In addition to this he receives impressions from past activities and, most important, he himself, being close to a total knowingness, conceives things about the past and future which are independent of immediately present stimuli. The mind is not in its entirety a stimulus-response mechanism as old Marxist psychology, as once taught in universities, would have one believe. The mind has three main divisions. The first of these could be called the *analytical mind,* the second the *reactive mind* and the third the *somatic mind.*

THE ANALYTICAL MIND

The *analytical mind* combines perceptions of the immediate environment, of the past (via pictures) and estimations of the future into conclusions which are based upon the realities of situations. The analytical mind combines the potential knowingness of the thetan with the conditions of his surroundings and brings him to independent conclusions. This mind could be said to consist of visual pictures either of the past or of the physical universe, monitored by, and presided over by, the knowingness of a thetan. The keynote of the analytical mind is awareness. One knows what one is concluding and knows what he is doing.

THE REACTIVE MIND

The *reactive mind* is a stimulus-response mechanism, ruggedly built, and operable in trying circumstances. The reactive mind never stops operating. Pictures, of a very low order, are taken by this mind of the environment even in some states of unconsciousness. The reactive mind acts below the level of consciousness. *It* is the literal, stimulus-response mind. Given a certain stimulus it gives a certain response. The entire subject of Dianetics concerned itself mainly with this one mind.

While it is an order of thinkingness, the ability of the reactive mind to conclude rationally is so poor that we find in the reactive mind those various aberrated impulses which are gazed upon as oddities of personality, eccentricities, neuroses and psychoses. It is this mind which stores up all the bad things that have happened to one and throws them back to him again in moments of emergency or danger so as to dictate his actions along lines which have been considered "safe" before. As there is little thinkingness involved in this, the courses of action dictated by the reactive mind are often not safe, but highly dangerous.

The reactive mind is entirely literal in its interpretation of words and actions. As it takes pictures and receives impressions during moments of unconsciousness, a phrase uttered when a blow is struck is likely to be literally interpreted by the reactive mind and becomes active upon the body and analytical mind at later times. The mildest stage of this would be arduous training, wherein a pattern is laid into the mind for later use under certain given stimuli.

A harsh and less workable level is the hypnotic trance condition to which the mind is susceptible. Made impressionable by fixed attention, words can be immediately implanted into the reactive mind which become operable under restimulation at later times.

An even lower level in the reactive mind is that one associated with blows, drugs, illness, pain and other conditions of unconsciousness. Phrases spoken over an anesthetized person can have a later effect upon that person. It is not necessarily true that each and every portion of an operation is painstakingly "photographed" by the reactive mind of the unconscious patient, but it is true that a great many of these stimuli are registered. Complete silence, in the vicinity of a person under anesthetic or a person who is unconscious or in deep pain, is mandatory if one would preserve the mental health of that person or patient afterwards.

Probably the most therapeutic action which could occur to an individual would be, under Scientology processing, the separation of the thetan from the mind so that the thetan, under no duress and with total knowingness, could view himself and his mind and act accordingly. However, there is a type of exteriorization which is the most aberrative of all traumatic actions. This is the condition when an individual is brought, through injury or surgery or shock, very close to death so that he exteriorizes from body and mind. This exteriorization under duress is sudden, and to the patient inexplicable, and is in itself very shocking. When this has occurred to an individual, it is certain that he will suffer mentally from the experience afterwards.

It could be said that when the reactive mind contains these sudden shocks of exteriorization under duress, attempts to exteriorize the individual later by Scientology are more difficult. However, modern processing has overcome this. The phenomenon of exteriorization under duress is accompanied at times by energy explosions in the various facsimiles of the mind, and these cross-associate in the reactive mind. Therefore, people become afraid of exteriorization, and at times people are made ill simply by discussing the phenomenon, due to the fact that they have exteriorized under duress during some operation or accident.

Exteriorization under duress is the characteristic of death itself. Therefore, exteriorization or the departure of the soul is generally associated with death in the minds of most people. It is not necessarily true that one is dead because he exteriorizes, and it is definitely not true that exteriorization not accompanied by a shock, pain or duress is at all painful. Indeed, it is quite therapeutic.

THE SOMATIC MIND

The third portion of the mind is the *somatic mind*. This is an even heavier type of mind than the reactive mind since it contains no thinkingness and contains only actingness. The impulses placed against the body by the thetan through various mental machinery arrive at the voluntary, involuntary and glandular levels. These have set methods of analysis for any given situation and so respond directly to commands given.

Unfortunately the somatic mind is subject to each of the minds higher in scale above it and to the thetan. In other words, the thetan can independently affect the somatic mind. The analytical mind can affect the somatic mind. The reactive mind can affect the somatic mind. Thus we see that the neurons, the glandular system, the muscles and masses of the body are subject to various impulses, each one of a lower order than the next. Thus it is not odd to discover what we call "psychosomatic" illness. A condition exists here where the thetan does not have an awareness of burdening the somatic mind with various commands or derangements. Neither does the thetan have an awareness of his own participation in the analytical mind causing this action against the body.

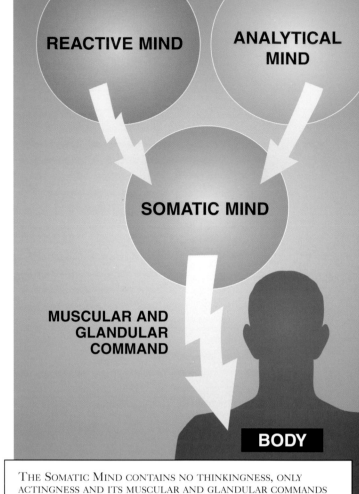

THE SOMATIC MIND CONTAINS NO THINKINGNESS, ONLY ACTINGNESS AND ITS MUSCULAR AND GLANDULAR COMMANDS CAN BE INFLUENCED BY THE REACTIVE OR ANALYTICAL MIND.

In that the thetan is seldom aware of the reactive mind, it is possible, then, for the reactive mind, with its stimulus-response content, to impinge itself directly, and without further recourse or advice, upon the neurons, muscles and glandular system of the body. In that the reactive mind can hold a fixed command in place, causing a derangement in the somatic mind, it is possible, then, for illness to exist, for bizarre pains to be felt, for actual physical twists and aberrations to occur, without any conscious knowledge on the part of the thetan. This we call physical illness caused by the mind. In brief, such illness is caused by perceptions received in the reactive mind during moments of pain and unconsciousness.

Whether the facsimile in the mind is received while the thetan is awake or unconscious, the resulting mass of the energy picture is energy just as you see energy in an electric light bulb or from the flames of a fire. At one time it was considered that mental energy was different from physical energy. In Scientology it has been discovered that mental energy is simply a finer, higher level physical energy. The test of this is conclusive in that a thetan "mocking up" [creating] mental image pictures and thrusting them into the body can increase the body mass and, by casting them away again, can decrease the body mass. This test has actually

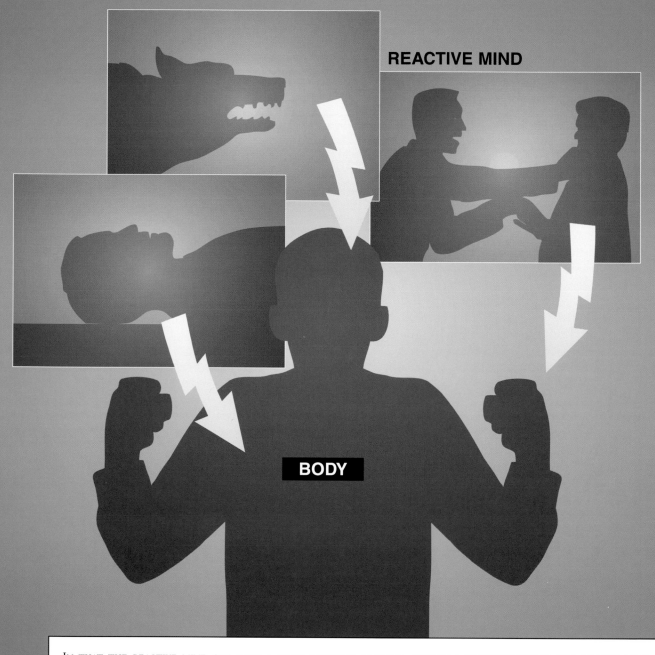

REACTIVE MIND

BODY

In that the reactive mind can hold a fixed command in place, causing a derangement in the somatic mind, it is possible then for illness to exist, for bizarre pains to be felt, for actual physical twists and aberrations to occur, without any conscious knowledge on the part of the thetan. This we call physical illness caused by the mind. In brief, such illness is caused by perceptions received in the reactive mind during moments of pain and unconsciousness.

been made and an increase of as much as thirty pounds, actually measured on scales, has been added to, and subtracted from, a body by creating "mental energy." Energy is energy. It has different wavelengths and different characteristics. The mental image pictures are capable of reacting upon the physical environment, and the physical environment is capable of reacting upon mental image pictures. Thus the mind actually consists of spaces, energies and masses of the same order as the physical universe, if lighter and different in size and wavelength. For a much more comprehensive picture of the mind one should read *The Dynamics of Life* and *Dianetics: The Modern Science of Mental Health*. These were written before the discoveries of the upper levels of beingness were made and are a very

complete picture of the mind itself, its structure and what can be done to it and with it.

THE BODY

The third part of man is the physical *body*. This can best be studied in such books as *Gray's Anatomy* and other anatomical texts. This is the province of the medical doctor and, usually, the old-time psychiatrist or psychologist, who were involved, in the main, in body worship. The body is a purely structural study, and the actions and reactions among its various structures are complex and intensely interesting.

When Scientology established biophysics, it did so because of the various discoveries which had accumulated concerning mental energy in its reaction against physical energy, and the activities which took place in the body because of these interactions. Biophysics only became feasible when it was discovered in Scientology that a fixed electrical field existed surrounding a body entirely independent of, but influenceable by, the human mind. The body exists in its own space. That space is created by *anchor points* [those points which demark (limit) the outermost boundaries of a space or its corners]. The complexity of these anchor points can cause an independent series of electronic flows which can occasion much discomfort to the individual. The balance structure of the body and even its joint action and physical characteristics can be changed by changing this electrical field which exists at a distance from, or within, the body.

The electrical field is paramount and monitors the actual physical structure of the body. Thus the body is not only influenced by the three minds, it is influenced as well by its own electrical field. An expert Scientologist can discover for the average person this field, and can bring about its adjustment, although this is very far from the primary purpose of the Scientologist.

The use of electrical shocks upon a body for any purpose is therefore very dangerous and is not condoned by sensible men. Of course, the use of electrical shock was never intended to be therapeutic, but was intended only to bring about obedience by duress and, as far as it can be discovered, to make the entirety of insanity a horror. Electrical shock deranges the electronic field in the vicinity of the body and is always succeeded by bad health or physical difficulties and never does otherwise than hasten the death of the person. It has been stated by people using electric shock that if they were denied euthanasia they would at least use partial euthanasia in the form of electric shock, brain surgery and drugs. These treatments in some large percentage of cases, however, effected euthanasia as they were expected to do.

A knowledge of the mental and physical structure of the body would be necessary in order to treat the body, and this knowledge has not existed prior to Scientology. The medical doctor achieved many results by working purely with structure and biochemical products, and in the field of emergency surgery and obstetrics and orthopedics, he is indispensable in the society. Medicine, however, did not even contain a definition for *mind* and is not expected to invade the field which belongs properly to Scientology.

These three parts of man—the thetan, the mind and the body—are each one different studies, but they influence each other markedly and continually. Of the three, the senior entity is the thetan, for without the thetan there would be no mind or animation in the body, while without a body or a mind there is still animation and life in the thetan. The thetan *is* the person. You are *you*, *in* a body.

Many speculations in the field of para-Scientology have been made. Para-Scientology includes all of the uncertainties and unknown territories of life which have not been completely explored and explained. However, as studies have gone forward, it has become more and more apparent that the senior activity of life is that of the thetan, and that in the absence of the spirit no further life exists. In the insect kingdom it is not established whether or not each insect is ordered by a spirit or whether one spirit orders enormous numbers of insects. It is not established how mutation and evolution occur (if they do), and the general authorship of the physical universe is only speculated upon, since Scientology does not invade the eighth dynamic.

Some facts, however, are completely known. The first of these is that the individual himself is a spirit controlling a body via a mind. The second of these is that the thetan is capable of making space, energy, mass and time. The third of these is that the thetan is separable from the body without the phenomenon of death, and can handle and control a body from well outside it. The fourth of these is that the thetan does not care to remember the life which he has just lived, after he has parted from the body and the mind. The fifth of these is that a person dying always exteriorizes. The sixth of these is that the person, having exteriorized, usually returns to a planet and procures, usually, another body of the same type of race as before.

In para-Scientology there is much discussion about *between-lives areas* and other phenomena which might have passed at one time or another for heaven or hell, but it is established completely that a thetan is immortal and that he

Psychosomatic Illness

70% PSYCHO- SOMATIC

Seventy percent of all illnesses are diagnosed as having mental causes, indicating the tremendous effect the mind has on a person's well-being. Current medical practice attempts to treat these with physical means only.

THE THETAN IS CAPABLE OF MAKING SPACE, ENERGY, MASS AND TIME.

himself cannot actually experience death and counterfeits it by forgetting. It is adequately manifest that a thetan lives again and that he is very anxious to put something on the *time track* (something for the future) in order to have something to come back to, thus we have the anxieties of sex. There must be additional bodies for the next life.

It is obvious that what we create in our societies during this lifetime affects us during our next lifetime. This is quite different than the "belief," or the idea, that this occurs. In Scientology we have very little to do with forcing people to make conclusions. An individual can experience these things for himself and unless he can do so no one expects him to accept them.

The manifestation that our hereafter is our next life entirely alters the general concept of spiritual destiny. There is no argument whatever with the tenets of faith since it is not precisely stated, uniformly, by religions that one immediately goes to a heaven or hell. It is certain that an individual experiences the effect of the civilization which he has had part in creating, in his next lifetime. In other words, the individual comes back. He has a responsibility for what goes on today since he will experience it tomorrow.

When discussing the phenomena of death, one is probably touching upon the single most universally pondered philosophic question. Moreover, and particularly what with a doubling of an American population beyond the age of sixty-five, one is discussing a matter of truly grave concern. In reply to all that death represents as the grand promise of a hereafter (or what with the advent of the scientific age, the grand extinction), stands L. Ron Hubbard's "The Phenomena of Death."

By way of introduction, let us briefly return to late 1951, when on the heels of Dianetics, Ron declared: "The further one investigated, the more one came to understand that here, in this creature *Homo sapiens,* were entirely too many unknowns." In particular, he cited "strange yearnings" for faraway lands, curious memories of distant times, and those with no observable training, suddenly, and quite inexplicably, speaking foreign tongues. Then, too, and herein lay the crux, there were cases soon on record, dozens actually, wherein those receiving Dianetics had not shown expected improvement until traumatic experience from what appeared to have been several lifetimes had been alleviated.

To appreciate what was unfolding, let us understand that if Dianetics involves "the tracing of experience" to discharge buried trauma, then it was found to be incumbent upon the Dianetics auditor to address the whole of that experience—even including, as Ron explained, "phenomena for which we have no adequate explanation." His first recorded statement on the matter was equally indeterminate. In reference to a case wherein remarkably convincing details of an apparently former death were offered, he very simply remarked, "We have to keep an open mind about these things," and would not further commit himself. Privately, however, he seems to have remained unconvinced, and reasonably suggested the so-called former life sequence to be imaginative, perhaps representing a means of "taking refuge in a fictitious past." But in either case, and to this he held firm, the matter clearly warranted further investigation.

To grasp what next ensued requires a short explanation of circumstances. Not long after the publication of *Dianetics: The Modern Science of Mental Health,* and in the wake of unprecedented popularity (the book soon topped best-seller lists, generated banner headlines and finally inspired nothing short of a national movement) the first Dianetics Research Foundation had formed in Elizabeth, New Jersey. Although nominally listed among the directors, Ron confined himself to further research, lectures and the training of students. The actual administration of Foundation affairs fell to others, and within that arrangement, he found himself facing a board resolution to prohibit any and all further discussion of past lives.

If one is to be entirely fair, those behind that now infamous New Jersey board resolution must not be accused of an arbitrary prejudice. After all, and particularly within mid-twentieth-century Western society, the notion of a former existence was nothing if not foreign. Moreover, when speaking of those from the New Jersey board, including the aforementioned Michigan physician Dr. Joseph Winter, former Western Electric engineer Donald Rogers and *Astounding Science Fiction* editor, John W. Campbell, Jr., one is speaking of quite a materially minded crew. Campbell, for example, had previously struggled with several elaborate theories to explain human thought in purely cellular terms, and was otherwise much concerned that Dianetics

remain on an acceptably scientific, i.e., material footing. Meanwhile, the just as politically concerned Winter, in his capacity as Foundation medical director, continued to argue that Dianetics would never gain true acceptance (and all-important federal funding) unless amalgamated into the American psychological and psychiatric establishment... Which, in turn, demanded nothing shake a psychological/psychiatric creed that defined our lives as a purely biochemical process beginning with our birth and ending with our death.

Much more might be said, including the fact that, quite in addition to a psychological/psychiatric aversion to evidence of past lives, a good part of Christian dogma stood opposed to the notion. The thinking is complex and quite deeply rooted in a Christian orthodoxy wherein the central appeal was a hope of *physical* resurrection. In brief, however, the argument is this: If, as suggested in various Gnostic scriptures, the human soul was destined to rebirth, then obviously the threat of eternal damnation tended to lose its sting. Which was not to say the sinner did not suffer under Gnostic doctrine. On the contrary, earth itself became the unending hell for those who lived, lifetime after lifetime, beyond the grace of God. Yet from a strictly ecumenical standpoint, a doctrine of reincarnation tended to undermine Church authority as the sole means of salvation and everlasting life through the grace of Christ. Moreover, it tended to undermine key sources of Church revenue, very much including the sale of indulgences. Consequently, came the formal expunging of all such doctrine with the Second Synod of Constantinople in 553 AD.

None of this, of course, figured into Ron's thinking. Rather, his concerns remained purely practical and solely determined by workability. Did those receiving auditing benefit from addressing what was perceived as traumatic experience from a former life or did they not? No other factor, whether political or philosophical, was deemed relevant. Besides which—and this in unqualified terms to members of the Foundation board—"You can't pass resolutions to say what is or isn't in the human mind."

Reprinted in the following pages is Ron's introductory note to what may be viewed as the culmination of such research, the 1960, *Have You Lived Before this Life?* The text is comprised of forty-two cases wherein advanced Scientology auditing procedures were employed to alleviate difficulties stemming from former lives. What those forty-two cases tell us in a larger philosophic context is, of course, monumental and bears upon the whole of our existence... including the startling proposition, as LRH so bluntly puts it, "what we create in our societies during this lifetime affects us during our next lifetime." Equally startling were the results of those Scientology auditing procedures; there are more than a few documented cases, for example, wherein hopelessly crippled polio victims were restored to full mobility after, and only after, addressing former lives. Finally, for those intrigued by such details, there was the subsequent case of a young Scientologist who recalled, not only the circumstances of her former life, but the actual place of her burial. Whereupon she made her way to a southern English churchyard and there, just as recalled through the course of her auditing, stood the otherwise forgotten gravestone bearing her former name. ▨

The Phenom
by L. Ron

It has only been in Scientology that the mechanics of death have been thoroughly understood. Hitherto, the whole subject of death has been one of the more mysterious subjects to man.

We are actually the first people that do know a great deal about death. It is one of the larger successes of Scientology.

In the first place, man is composed of a body, a mind and what we refer to as a *thetan*—the Scientology word for the spirit, the individual being himself who handles and lives in the body.

A very effective way to demonstrate this is by saying to a person, "Look at your body. Have you got a body there?" Then tell him, "Get a mental picture of a cat." He will get a picture of a cat. That picture is a mental image picture and is part of the mind.

The mind is composed of pictures that interassociate, act and carry perceptions. While the person is looking at this actual picture ask him, "What's looking at it?"

Nobody ever asked this question before! It is quite an innocent question, but this particular phrasing and this particular demonstration of the parts of man were unknown before Scientology.

This procedure gives a person a considerable

ena of Death
Hubbard

subjective reality on the idea that he himself is a being that is independent of a mind or a body. There is an actual separateness there.

Man thought he *had* a human spirit. That is totally incorrect. Man *is* a human spirit which is enwrapped more or less in a mind which is in a body. That is *Homo sapiens*. He is a spirit and his usual residence is in his head. He looks at his mental image pictures and his body carries him around.

What happens to man when he dies?

Basically, all that happens is that a separation occurs between the thetan and the body.

The thetan, however, takes with him old tin cans, rattling chains, bric-a-brac and other energy phenomena that he feels he cannot do without and stashes this in the next body that he picks up.

In this lazy time of manufactured items and gadgetry he does not build a new body. He picks up a body that is produced according to a certain blueprint that has been carried through from the earliest times of life on this planet until now.

There is such a thing as a cycle of action: create-survive-destroy. At the shoulder of the curve an individual is mostly interested in surviving. Early on the curve he is interested in creating. And at the end of the curve, he is interested in the disposition of the remains.

This cycle of action occurs whether you are speaking of a building, a tree or anything else. When we apply this cycle of action to the parts of man, we get a death of the body, a partial death of the mind and a condition of forgetting on the part of the spiritual being which is in itself a type of death.

The first thing one should learn about death is that it is not anything of which to be very frightened. If you are frightened of losing your pocketbook, if you are frightened of losing your memory, if you are frightened of losing your girl or your boyfriend, if you are frightened of losing your body—well that is how frightened you ought to be of dying, because it is all the same order of magnitude.

We strike the first observable phenomenon in death when we find out that the mind, in spite of mechanisms which seek to decay it and wipe it out, does maintain and preserve mental image pictures of earlier existences. And with proper technology and an understanding of this one can be again possessed of the mental image pictures of earlier existences in order to understand what was going on.

But unless *remembrance* is restored to the *being*, the mental image pictures usually just continue to be pictures. Without that remembrance, sending somebody into a past life and having him look at a mental image picture would be similar to sending him to the art gallery. He would not connect himself with that picture.

The restoration of memory is therefore of great interest, since all that is really *wrong* with a person is that things have

happened to him which he knows all about, but won't let himself in on.

The restoration of memory is done as a matter of course in almost any Dianetics or Scientology processing. It is impossible today to process somebody well and expertly without having them sooner or later get recall with reality on a past existence.

Past lives can be easily invalidated because, without processing, it is difficult to remember them. An individual's own will has a great deal to do with this. One should not look for outside sources as to why his memory is shut off. Just as he must grant permission to be trapped, so must he grant permission to be made to remember. He is more or less convinced that a memory, remembering back past this subject called death, would cause him to reexperience the pain he already feels has been too much for him. Thus he is very reluctant to face up again to this mechanism, and in facing death almost always goes into a degree of amnesia.

Now, it is all very well to take a scientific attitude towards death, but after all it does carry with it a little shock and upset. Until you have been dead a few times you wouldn't understand how upsetting it can be!

We are actually indebted for a considerable amount of our material on this subject to the odd fact that I have been officially dead twice in this lifetime. I died in an operation one time back in the 1930s, and went outside above the street, felt sorry for myself and decided they couldn't do this to me. The body's heart had stopped beating, and I went back and grabbed the body through the mechanisms in the head that stimulate its heartbeats. I just took hold of them and snapped the body back to life.

The only reason I mention this is because it happens to so many people and they never mention it. They die and come back to life again. Then somebody invalidates them, and they never say anything about it again.

Ordinarily when a person dies, he backs out of his body thinking of his responsibilities, knowing who he is, where he has been and what he has been doing. If he is in any kind of condition at all this is what occurs. He backs out at the moment of death with full memory.

Something kills a person's body—an automobile, too many court suits, an overdose of widely advertised sleep-producing agents. The moment he conceives it to be no longer functional in any way, he backs out. Usually a total occlusion does not occur at this point.

It is not true that a thetan gets some distance from the body and then doesn't care about it anymore or forgets all about it. In support of this, incidents have been recorded of times when a thetan backed out of his head and was as mad as the dickens and just kicked the stuffings out of the fellow who had killed him. This made the whole theory of spirits very unpopular. People tried to forget this, so that when they ran around killing people they would get no immediate kickback. Some people would *want* to forget about it, thinking that in this way they could commit a crime without having to suffer for it.

Man has capitalized on the phenomena surrounding death enormously. Look around in any neighborhood—you will find that if there is any building which is well kept, it is normally an undertaking parlor. Why is it easy to capitalize on death?

Because when people think of death they think of loss and grab something.

Past lives, or times we have lived before, are suppressed by the painfulness of the memory of those former existences.

The memory is contained in mental image pictures which, on close viewing, are capable of developing a reality "more real" than present time.

Where a person has been tortured or killed without adequate reason, the injustice of it causes him or her to protest by holding in suspension in time the picture.

To restore the memory of one's whole existence, it is necessary to bring one up to being able to confront such experiences.

A person with amnesia is looked upon as ill. What of a person who can remember only this life? Is this then not a case of amnesia on a grand scale?

Psychosomatic illnesses such as arthritis, asthma, rheumatism, heart trouble, and on and on for a total of 70 percent of man's ills—and women's too—are the reaction of the body against a painful mental image picture or *engram*. When this picture is cleared away—if it is the right picture—the illness usually abates.

Actual fevers and pain, etc., can turn on just by restimulation of mental pictures in a person.

The recovery of whole memory could be said to be a goal of processing.

Past lives are "incredible" only to those who dare not confront them. In others, the fact of former existence can be quickly established subjectively.

There are many interesting cases on record since Dianetics gave impetus to Bridey Murphy. One was a case of a young girl, about five, who, hanging back at church, confided to her clergyman that she was worried about her "husband and

ON PAST LIVES

BY L. RON HUBBARD

children." It seems she had not forgotten them after "dying out of" another life five years before.

The clergyman did not at once send for the chaps in white coats. Instead, he questioned the truly worried child closely.

She told him she had lived in a nearby village, and what her name had been. She said where her former body was buried, gave him the address of her husband and children and what all their names were, and asked him to drive over and find out if they were all right.

The clergyman made the trip. Much to his astonishment, he discovered the grave, the husband, the children and all the current news.

The following Sunday he told the little five-year-old girl that the children were all well, that the husband had remarried pleasantly and that the grave was well kept.

She was very satisfied and thanked the clergyman very much—and the following Sunday could not recall a thing about it!

Past lives are not the same as the theory which has been called "reincarnation" in Hinduism. That is a complex theory compared to simply living time after time, getting a new body, eventually losing it and getting a new one.

The facts of past lives, if you care to pursue them, are best seen from a preclear's viewpoint in the hands of a competent auditor. The hypnotic handling of such is not advised. Only by higher levels of awareness does one learn, not deeper levels of unconsciousness.

An amusing sidelight on past lives is the "famous person" fixation. This more than anything else has discredited having lived before. There is always some madman "who was Napoleon," always some girl "who was Catherine the Great." This evidently means that the person, living a contemporary life to a famous figure, was so unsuccessful that he or she "dubbed in" the great personage. An auditor who runs into "Beethoven," after the preclear has run it for a while, finds the preclear was really the handler of a street piano in that life—not Beethoven!

But all rules have exceptions, and an auditor once found a preclear who claimed to have been Jim Bowie, the famous frontiersman who died at the doubly famous Alamo in Texas. And after much work and great skepticism found he really did have Jim Bowie!

People have also been animals and perhaps some animals have been people. There evidently is no gradient scale of advance, as in the theories of reincarnation, but there are cases on record of preclears who got well after a life as a dog or other animal was run out by an auditor.

One case, a psychotic girl, recovered when a life as a lion who ate his keeper was fully run out!

And we have also known horses and dogs of "human intelligence." Perhaps they had just been generals or ministers of state and were taking it easy for a life or two to cure their ulcers!

Viewing children in the light of knowledge of past lives causes us to revise our estimations of causes of child behavior.

Evidently the newborn child has just died as an adult. Therefore he or she, for some years, is prone to fantasy and terror and needs a great deal of love and security to recover a perspective of life with which he or she can live.

Life is never dull in the researches and practice of Dianetics and Scientology. The motto is—*What is*, *is*, not what we wished it were.

This explains the behavior of relatives after one of their family has died. Everybody gets in there and tears apart all of the person's clothes and they fight with each other over the possessions. They are still alive, but they have experienced a loss of havingness and they pore over this particular person's effects. They are really to some degree trying to get the person back. They think if they can grab enough possessions, they will get the person back. It actually is not quite as greedy as it looks, it is just obsessive.

I have seen relatives, for instance, pick up some of the weirdest things. I once saw an old lady just screaming over the fact that someone wouldn't let her have a fellow's meerschaum pipe. I pointed out to her that she didn't smoke a meerschaum pipe, and she looked at me sort of dazedly and came out of it and said, "So I don't," and handed it to somebody else. It was a token, a symbol of the person who had just left.

The exact behavior at death could vary from person to person. A person who had to "have" tremendously would get just so far from a body and be liable to say, "I don't care, I don't want to live anyway, I was very unhappy during that whole life and I'm awfully glad I don't care."

Somebody else is just as liable to not even think about it. But that person was so little alive, when he was alive, that his aliveness after he has died is also negligible.

With a person who is fairly strong and capable there is an interesting reaction to body death: "I'll show them they can't put me out of the game." It makes him mad and upsets him, and he does a dive halfway across the country, sees a maternity hospital and grabs a baby body.

The exteriorization which occurs at death is very fascinating because the person is totally cognizant of it. He knows who he is; he usually has pretty good perception; he knows where his friends are. Pointing out as a fantastic spiritual phenomenon the occurrence of somebody appearing to a friend after he had died several thousand miles away, is something like being very surprised because a waitress came to the table in a restaurant.

People also sometimes wake up during the night and realize that somebody has died a death of violence. This is usually because of the amount of confusion which is thrown into a being when his body is killed. If a person is killed with sudden violence and is very surprised about it, he can be sufficiently upset and unphilosophical about the whole thing that he is liable to go around and see his next of kin and the rest of his friends in an awful frenzied hurry, trying to reassure himself that he hasn't gone to purgatory or someplace.

He has suffered a loss of mass. If you had an automobile sitting out on the street and you went out totally expecting to find the automobile there and it was gone, you would be upset. That is just about the frame of mind a thetan is usually in when he finds his body dead. His main thought is to grasp another body. This he could do by finding a young child that he could bring back to life.

But the ordinary entrance of a thetan into a new body is sometime around what we call the *assumption,* and the assumption occurs within a few minutes after birth in most cases. The baby is born and then a thetan picks up the baby body.

How do thetans behave when they suddenly haven't got a body? They behave like people. They will hang around people. They will see a woman who is pregnant and follow her down the street. Or they will hang around the entrance to an accident ward and find some body that is all banged up and the being that had that body has taken off or is about to. He may even pick up this body and pretend to be somebody's husband.

Thetans do all sorts of odd things. *When* a new body is picked up, if a new body is picked up at all, is not standardized beyond saying it usually occurs (unless the thetan got another idea) two or three minutes after the delivery of a child from the mother. A thetan usually picks it up about the time the baby takes its first gasp.

Would the body go on living without a thetan picking it up? That is beside the point. It is a case of how fast the thetan can pick one up before somebody else gets it. There is a certain anxiety connected with this.

Thetans often say very interesting prayers at the moment they pick up a body. They dedicate themselves to its continued growing and to the family and go through all kinds of odd rituals, all because they are so happy to get a new body. But the odd part of it is, they don't shut their memory off until they pick another body up. The shut-off of memory actually occurs with the pickup of the new body.

Death is in itself a technical subject. You can, with considerable confidence, reassure some husband whose wife has just died that she got out all right and she is going someplace to take up a new body. If you got there while that person could still communicate with you, in the last moments, you would find that the person usually has something spotted, something planned.

The person doesn't just back out ordinarily and forget all about it. He backs out of it with full identity and hangs around for quite a while. The being is usually there for the funeral, certainly. He will very often hang around his possessions to see that they are not abused, and he can be given upsets if his wishes aren't carried out with regard to certain things.

It used to happen that thetans would punish people for not carrying out their wishes after death. People then said this was superstition, and science was against superstition. Well, it is quite interesting that in finding out what is science and what is superstition, we have found that a being is

capable of almost anything providing it is within his ability to execute.

Losing your pocketbook, some treasured possession or your body are all alike. But because of the mechanism of forgetting, a great mystery is made of this.

And that is death, phenomena of.

With a recognition of our immortality, our essential goodness and inherent capabilities, Scientology became "a religious philosophy in its highest meaning as it brings man to total freedom and truth." It may be further defined as, "the study and handling of the spirit in relationship to itself, universes and other life," and comprises "a wisdom in the tradition of ten thousand years of search in Asia and in Western civilization."

Beyond these statements, no intellectual appreciation is sufficient. Given a thousand years of Christian doctrine, it is easy enough to form some conception of a Christian heaven. While given the preponderance of the twentieth-century scientific theory, it is even easier to imagine our lives in strictly material terms—striving for reasonable happiness until the neural cortex breaks down and we are plunged into absolute unconsciousness forever. But without some subjective experience, even L. Ron Hubbard, in this perfectly succinct 1966 explanation, can only suggest the "tremulous wonder" of all Scientology offers.

Dianetics, Scientology & Beyond

by L. Ron Hubbard

For thousands of years men have sought the state of complete spiritual freedom from the endless cycle of birth and death and have sought personal immortality containing full awareness, memory and ability as a spirit independent of the flesh.

The dream of this in Buddha's time was called "Bodhi," being the name of the tree under which he attained such a state.

But due to the unknown presence of the reactive mind and its effect upon the spirit as well as the body, such periods of freedom were difficult to attain and were, as we have found, temporary.

Further, few could attain even this temporary state and those who did acquired it at the cost of decades of self-denial and personal discipline.

In Scientology this state has been attained. It has been achieved not on a temporary basis, subject to relapse, but on a stable plane of full awareness and ability, unqualified by accident or deterioration. And not limited to a few.

By eradicating the reactive mind we not only achieve in the state of Clear an erasure of the seeming evil in man, who is basically good, we have overcome the barriers which made it so difficult to attain total spiritual independence and serenity.

We call this state "Operating Thetan." To *operate* something is to be able to handle it. *Thetan* is from the Greek letter "theta" the traditional philosopher's symbol (from the letter in the Greek alphabet "theta" θ) of thought, spirit or life. Thus it means a being who as a spirit alone can handle things.

The definition of the state of Operating Thetan is "Knowing and willing cause over Life, Thought, Matter, Energy, Space and Time."

As man is basically good, despite his evil reactions to his reactive mind, a being who is Clear becomes willing to trust himself with such abilities. And in any case none can have more power than they can control.

In Scientology a Clear can walk his way to Operating Thetan, not in the decades demanded even by a temporary state in past ages, but within months or at most a year or so. And when he attains the state he is no longer subject to sudden and inexplicable collapses as occurred 2,500 years ago. One is able to attain and retain the desirable condition.

Not the least of the qualities of OT is personal and knowing immortality and freedom from the cycle of birth and death.

The concept is rather vast for immediate grasp but chiefly because one has hoped and had his hope for this turned to despair and his despair turned to a total apathy concerning it too often down the ages to do more than extend a tremulous wonder.

But the way is true and plainly marked and all one needs to do is to place his feet upon the first rung of the ladder of Dianetics, ascend by Scientology to Clear and then walk upward to and far beyond the stars.

It is quite impossible to overstate the importance of such news. 2,500 years ago a statement similar to this and almost impossible to attain brought civilization to three-quarters of Asia.

Yet day by day, Clears enrolled on the "OT Course" are walking that ladder and have already begun to reach the stars.

It is quite true. And quite attainable on the well-marked road of modern Scientology.

Philosophy, L. Ron Hubbard explains, is the pursuit of wisdom. It is something we use to think with, to wonder with, to accept or reject. In what amounts to a definitive statement of Scientology's place within that tradition comes Ron's "Philosophy Wins After 2000 years." Although self-explanatory, a few incidental notes might be supplied: In referencing the Greeks—Aristotle, Socrates, Plato and Euclid, in particular—he is acknowledging those he had long viewed as legitimate predecessors of Dianetics and Scientology. That he chose to make such a statement in 1965 is especially significant; for it was through this period he commenced the mapping of the route to Operating Thetan, or that realm, as he elsewhere described it, "not even embraced by earlier literature." Finally, we might wish to bear in mind yet another LRH word on Scientology: "It is a religious philosophy, but it is a philosophy. And that it is something you use to think with, to wonder with, to accept or reject."

Philosophy Wins After 2000 Years

By L. Ron Hubbard

Photograph by L. Ron Hubbard

Philosophy did not die with Ancient Greece. Out of the natural philosophy of those times came science. The wonders of chrome and metal cars, planes, the atom bomb and even satellites have their roots in the firm base of Greek philosophy. But Socrates, Aristotle, Euclid, Thales, Heraclitus, Parmenides, Democritus, Pythagoras, Plato, Anaxagoras, Lucretius and all the rest did not have in mind the manufacture of material things when they released their knowledge to the world.

Even though all these great things developed out of Greek thought and mathematics, the great names of philosophy considered they had failed.

And so they had. Until today.

For their philosophic goal was the understanding of the spirit of man and his relationship to the universe. And they could only speculate upon it. They never proved their contention that man was a spirit clothed in flesh, they could only assert it.

And so they drowned in the avalanche of superstition which engulfed the world in the Dark Ages.

Why did they fail? They needed the higher mathematics and electronics which would, over two thousand years later, develop their philosophies.

These were developed. But they were used for different purposes than those intended, and man turned his back upon their lofty dreams while building planes to bomb cities and atom bombs to wipe out the mankind no one had ever understood.

Until Scientology.

And in it the goals of Greek philosophy live again.

Using modern developments in the sciences, it became possible to approach again the basic problems: What is man? What is his relationship to the universe? What is the universe?

Scientology, after a third of a century of careful research and investigation can answer, with scientific truth those questions and prove the answers. This is rather startling.

We have come so far from Thales, Heraclitus, Parmenides and Democritus that we have almost forgotten what they were trying to discover. But if you consult writings of the work they did over two thousand years ago you will see what it was.

They wanted man to know. They did not fail. They laid the ancient Greeks a firm foundation on which to build. And two thousand and more years later we can furnish all the evidence they need.

And that evidence and its truths and its great potential of betterment for the individual and all mankind are completed work today in Scientology.

We have reached the star they saw. And we know what it is. You'll find its value when you become a Scientologist, a being who has come to know himself, life and the universe and can give a hand to those around him to reach the stars.

Scientology Answers

Man has asked a great many questions about himself.

Such questions are "Who am I?" "Where do I come from?" "What is death?" "Is there a hereafter?"

Any child asks these questions, yet man has never had answers that long satisfied him.

Religions have various answers to these questions and they belong in fact in the field of religious philosophy, since this is the area of man's knowledge that has sought to answer them.

Answers have varied through the ages and race to race and this variation alone is the stumbling block which brings disbelief into faiths. Old religions fade because people no longer find their answers to the above questions real.

The decline of Christianity is marked by modern cynicism about a Hell where one burns for an eternity and a Heaven where one plays a harp forever.

Materialistic sciences have sought to invalidate the entire field by shrugging the problem off with the equally impossible answers that one is merely meat and all life arose by spontaneous and accidental combustion from a sea of ammonia. Such "answers" sound more like pre-Buddhist India where the world was said to be carried on seven pillars that stood on seven pillars which stood on a turtle and, in exasperation to the child's question as to what the turtle stood on, "Mud! And it's mud from there on down!"

Photograph by L. Ron Hubbard

It is the nature of truth that if one knows it, even more things get understood. The disease and decay of Asia tend to invalidate their concepts as truth and in the West, war, where soldiers saw *"Gott Mit Uns"* [God is with us] on the slain enemy belt buckles tended to end the domination of the churches of those times—for God could not be on both sides of such Devil's work, or so the soldiers reasoned.

Even Christ's great commandment of "Love thy neighbor" seems to have less force today in a world of income tax, inflation and the slaughter of civil populations in the name of peace.

So without in any way condemning or scorning any man's beliefs, Scientology arose from the ashes of a spiritless science and again asked—and answered—the eternal questions. That the answers have the force of truth is attested by the results. Instead of the sickness of religious India, Scientologists are seldom ill. Instead of internal warfare such as the riots of Alexandria, Scientologists live in relative harmony with each other and have skills that restore relations rapidly.

The world tends to attack new things and Scientology has had its share from vested interest groups and governments but it keeps rising eventually victorious from each clash without bitterness.

Various interesting results proceed from the practice of Scientology. One's intelligence increases and one's ability to handle his problems is markedly bettered. One does not have to study Scientology very long to know that one does not have to die to find out what he is or where he is going after death, for *one can experience* it all for himself with no persuasion or hypnotism or "faith."

So Scientology is different mainly because one doesn't have to *believe* in it to have it work. Its truths are of the order of "Is this black?" "Is this white?" You can

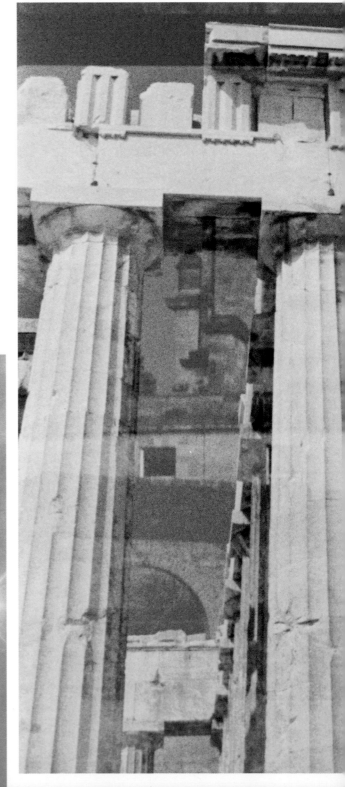

Photographs by L. Ron Hubbard

see for yourself something is black if it's black and that something is white when it's white. No tricks of logic are needed to prove any point and Scientologists only ask people to look for themselves. Thus, along with science, Scientology can achieve positive invariable results. Given the same conditions, one always gets the same results. And anyone given the same conditions can obtain the same results.

What has happened is the *superstition* has been subtracted from spiritual studies. And today this is a very acceptable state of affairs to man.

The ultimate freedom depends on knowing the ultimate truth. Truth is not what people *say* it is, it is what it *is*. And truth, quite remarkably, sets one free, just like philosophers have said down the ages.

What the philosopher did *not* say was how free can one get? And that is the surprise contained in Scientology for everyone who walks the road to truth—one *can* be totally free.

Naturally this makes no friendly news to the person who wants slaves, and fascistic, capitalistic and even some more liberal creeds forbid that utterly, for who could be a master, so they think, where no slave wears his chains? They miss the point entirely, for who *has* to be a master?

When you yourself hold the truth, the shadows by which you are bound tend to slither away.

And when you at last know for yourself in your own experience that Scientology does have the answers, and when you have applied them, you have the result all philosophers, savants, sages and saviors have always dreamed of—and freedom as well.

As much of Scientology is true for you as you know of it; those who know it only by name react to the hope of it. And as one advances upon the road, one knows more and more of it and is more and more free. Unlike so many promises made to man and which have made him fear disappointment, Scientology delivers. It may be over a rough road. It may be over a smooth one. But Scientology eventually delivers all it says it can.

And that is what is new about it and why it grows. No other religion ever given man, delivered. They all waited until after the end for one to find his harp or his Nirvana.

For the first time in all the ages there *is* something that within one lifetime delivers the answers to the eternal questions and delivers immortality as well.

When considering all Dianetics and Scientology represent as both a philosophic statement and a means to the realization of that statement, it is only reasonable to assume L. Ron Hubbard would have met with opposition. In the simplest terms, he speaks of a "power elite" made uneasy with a genuinely popular philosophic movement, and particularly one which stands so unequivocally for individual freedom. He also speaks of what Dianetics and Scientology represent to an international psychiatric establishment and financially linked pharmaceutical industry (both of which have traditionally stood at loggerheads to the spiritual, with a behavioral creed from Darwin and epitomized by Pavlov's "Philosophy of the Mechanistic"). Finally, and herein lies the rub, LRH speaks of a thirty-year psychiatric effort, not to bury his work, but to grab it.

The record bears him out. Among the several million pages of documentation eventually released from United States' government files are thousands of pages detailing attempts, both covert and overt, to appropriate Dianetics and Scientology for psychiatric offices within the American intelligence community. To what ends LRH discoveries were to be employed is not entirely clear, but the psychiatric obsession—the only word for it—is absolutely undisputable. Leafing through since declassified Central Intelligence Agency memoranda, for example, one repeatedly encounters suggestions of dark plans to first discredit and then appropriate the materials of Scientology. Likewise one encounters much in the way of attempted infiltration initiated by and on behalf of the Federal Bureau of Investigation, while illegally obtained copies of LRH lectures on the state of OT are still said to reside within National Security Agency vaults.

In reply, and remembering we are still speaking of a philosophic dispute, comes L. Ron Hubbard's "My Only Defense for Having Lived." It dates from 1966, or when several British and United States intelligence services conspired to curtail both Ron's personal movements and the growth of Scientology as a whole. Deeply personal and immensely powerful, let us simply describe it as a statement from a man whose life cannot be divorced from the convictions of his philosophy.

MY ONLY DE

The only tests of a life well lived are: Did he do what he intended? And were people glad he lived?

People have often desired me to write an autobiography and while I would be perfectly willing to do so had I the time, I consider such a work, as I do myself, quite unimportant.

I have led an adventurous life and it would possibly be entertaining to read, but I doubt such a work would shed any background light on my researches and would not clarify my intentions or why I developed Dianetics and Scientology.

My motives have not been fame. I tried to give Dianetics, the entire work, to the American Medical Association and the American Psychiatric Association in 1949 and the AMA only said "Why should you?" and the APA said "If it is important we will hear of it."

I tried to avoid, until July 1950, saying I had personally done the research but then owned to it when I saw that unowned, it could be lost in its original form.

FENSE FOR HAVING LIVED
BY L. RON HUBBARD

My motives have not included amassing great wealth. The royalties of the first book, *Dianetics: The Modern Science of Mental Health*, were given to the first Foundation. So it is not wealth.

Power has not been my motive. I only held office in organizations to insist upon correct usage of the work, and this having been achieved sometime since, I resigned all directorships and retained only an honorary post.

Further, one cannot have more power than he himself already has as a being; so power by reason of position I consider pointless and a waste of time.

My motives are so hard to understand because they largely omit me from the equation. And self-centered men are not likely to understand such a thing since *they* know they would not forgo fame, wealth or power and so conceive that another would not.

To try to understand me or Scientology by recounting the adventures of my life is a rather unrelated action. I am myself not my adventures. I have gone through the world studying man in order to understand him and *he*, not my adventures in doing so, is the important thing.

I always operated on the somewhat naive idea that my life was my own, to be lived as best I could. A life is not always easy to live. When one's life becomes "public property" as mine seems to have done, one is ill prepared and not even inclined to explain it all. It has been lived, it cannot be unlived and there it is. The results of having lived at all, then, are the only things that count.

I never considered it worthwhile to live believably as that is a compromise which denies one's own integrity.

Also, to try to explain the technical inventions of a scientist by the way he plays a mandolin is of course something only a very dull person would do—yet of course people so try.

The trouble with my life is that it has been adventurous and would make, perhaps, interesting reading to lovers of adventure stories.

One does not study man successfully from an ivory tower

and part of my intentions has been to live a very full life in many strata so as to understand man. And this I have done.

I cannot say that I have liked all the things men do and say is necessary, but I can say that despite many reasons not to I have persevered in helping man all I could and continuing his friend.

Long since I ceased to talk about my real life. I learned long ago that man has his standards of credulity and when reality clashes with these he feels challenged.

For instance, I could read and write when I was three and a half. I could read minds and foretell the future with great accuracy. Such accomplishments startle people and I early learned in this lifetime to keep my own actual abilities to myself or else find sociability impossible.

I grew up on the frontier, amid brute force and the worship of brawn, learned to live in such a rough and tumble world, not die in forty below blizzards or lose my own standards in a barbarous society where agony was amusing to the people.

It carried its own legends and I had my adventures but I learned to tell the lesser tale.

No more than acclimatized in this lifetime to the old West, I found myself moved to the South Pacific and Asia, to a world of courtesy and soft ways and had to adopt a new pattern of survival.

This was no more than learned than I found myself, against my will, in the collegiate world studying engineering and mathematics, and learned new lessons in social contact. In this I was quite successful, becoming the head of various college clubs and societies. But in adapting a dead mathematics to new modern uses, I so assaulted the prejudices of my professors who thought dead mathematics should have no use that I learned once more about our world. I was ridiculed or frowned upon too often for writing or looking for the truth to ever conceive much love for the artificial towers of learning—so aloof from life. I decided to go study other races and organized an expedition and set sail in an old four-mast schooner rather than carry on longer in the academic world. I am amused to be condemned by some for not having studied in college a subject which was not taught there and which I had to develop to fill the gap in man's knowledge of himself. The answers did not exist in the books of philosophy I studied. It had to be looked for in the real world.

I wrote, I lived, I traveled, I prospered, I learned. I unfortunately could not quite help doing spectacular things. They would not look spectacular to me until I saw them in the eyes of others. And so I began to work very hard to tell the lesser tale, to do what I must to learn about man and help him as I could and yet not see wide-eyed disbelief, even shock, when someone at the Explorers Club would

introduce me as having roped a Kodiak bear, having climbed a volcano to see its eruption at close hand or as the doer of some other feat. I became cautious in my anecdotes but I was looking at and living life, in order to experience it, and what happened to me was entirely secondary.

When you see a student body of would-be writers almost mob you for saying factually you wrote a hundred thousand words a month as a quota, when you tell what is to you a simple truth and yet find others consider it extraordinary beyond belief you grow cautious about retelling the consecutive incidents which are your day by day life. You conclude others don't have a day by day life like that and so, not wanting to seem strange, you simply say less and when you do say you tell what you hope is ordinary and mildly entertaining.

Background for autobiography abounds. But who would read it as an honest tale and so I have not written it and never will. It would sound far, far too incredible. So I have abstained from writing vast tomes about myself and my adventures, not because I had done anything bad but because it was not important to do so and nobody would even believe my tales anyway.

Thus I have left a bit of mystery, unintentional, that others, with bad intent can fill in from their imaginations. I did not intend it so.

My intentions in life did not include making a story of myself. I only wanted to know man and understand him.

I did not really care if he did not understand me, so long as he understood himself. I was the lesser part of my project. Some say this is unfortunate, but I do not find it so. I did not live to be understood, but to understand.

And it does not matter. Long ago, I ceased utterly to defend myself against lies and calumny where it occurred. To some this will be considered strange. But how can one control the vaporings of a press which never interviews one?

Does one condemn and fight each rumor or lie?

I long ago realized I had not the time. But mainly I had not the inclination to stop man's speech and punish him for being what he was and for thinking what he did.

I learned early the folly of fighting the viciously inclined.

I was once expelled from an island, as a boy, by a gloomy and brooding governor, on a charge of always being happy and smiling. There was no more story than that.

So what does one do? Does one seek vengeance and death on men because they are ignorant, dull or intolerant?

Not when one's mission is to understand and help men.

Does one defend oneself against lies and infamy when one is already too busy doing his job?

One chooses what one is to do. And does it. All else is foolish distraction.

Threats to myself are unimportant in the scheme of things. I knew I would attain my goals. I knew it a long time ago.

I only once was frightened by the immensity of the implications of understanding man. It was when I had isolated in the late thirties what appeared to be the dynamic principle of existence and knew where such a discovery would lead.

I remembered man habitually crucified anyone who brought him wisdom or truly helped him.

I was frightened for a bit.

But I realized I had searched for an answer for too many years already to give up now. And then I accepted that condition. And have not halted on my way because of personal fear.

My life's history has no import. I have lived.

My only real regrets have been killing men in the thunder and passion of war and though I wish I had not, still it was done.

What people say I as a being have or have not done has

no bearing on the fact that my work has been done, done well and lives to help man become a better being. If I personally triumph for it or die for it in this life is not of the slightest possible importance.

What I have done for man's use cannot be undone by thousands of hostile columns of press or a hundred billion slanderous lies. My friends, and I have many, know they are lies, which is quite enough.

I am myself. I can hold up my head to myself. I know what I have done in developing a new philosophy and certainly I am not so foolish as to suppose it has no consequences for me. Only a fool would expect or value praise from the insane and not expect damage from the act of attempting to assist a wounded wild animal. One takes the consequences with the act.

I have carried out my basic intention—to understand man and help him attain greater heights of civilization through knowledge of himself.

And any friend I have and many, many more are glad that I have lived.

And that is the story of my life—the only story that matters.

My adventures, my heartbreaks, the joy I take in the singing wind and sea, my pride in creating prose and pictures, my attempts to compose music, my laughter with my friends and likes, dislikes and deeds are none of them discreditable.

So there have been attacks. Need this startle anyone? Such actions only prove that man needs help and needs it badly if he attacks his friends.

A past researched relentlessly for sixteen years by the world's press and even the police of a planet without the discovery of a single crime must be a singularly unstained past indeed!

Were you to read the press, up to 1950 . . .

I was a mildly famous, colorful person of excellent family, of unblemished repute, a member of famous clubs and societies, with many friends in high places.

On the publication of a book concerning the mind, I suddenly overnight was a dark villain with a terrible past (the crimes of course, unspecified, since there were none). From this we only learn that a person's own mind is apparently a monopoly somewhere, property of a sensitive group that profits too much to lose control. In any year thousands of books are written on philosophy and the mind, many banal, many vicious, many harmful, with no protest from anyone. Many of such works are by important people.

In any year thousands of self-betterment groups, good and evil, are formed without comment. Why then did the

publication of a book and the forming of a foundation cause such a fantastic reaction, all out of proportion to the importance of such usual acts?

Could it be because no special interest group had this new subject under their control? Could it be because the new subject had in it too much power of truth?

How is it that for sixteen years at this writing, the work, the groups, have continued and multiplied in the face of all opposition including that of governments (whose actions are startling, as who revolted against them)?

I sometimes feel like an old-time explorer, offering a balm to a pygmy mother for her baby's skin rash and being fearfully hunted by the tribe for "trying to put a spell on them." Ah well, explorers ran into that, didn't they?

With this much violence, had there been anything wrong with my past or with my current activities, I long since would have been done away with by the normal processes of law. But no, I remained untouched for all those sixteen years.

It has not been easy to live and work in a hostile atmosphere and yet protect my family and to carry on and keep faith with those who trusted me. I have borne it for the sake of others and for man.

It is interesting that all attempted actions against Scientology have eventually failed and have been proven falsely based in any court of law.

But who is this that is denounced by mighty figures of the press, by men of towering importance in the governments of the planet, who must be lied about and somehow put down? I as a person am not that important.

It doesn't make sense. And it makes less sense the more you consider it. For neither I nor the subject is an enemy of any of them.

Being easy in my own mind and sincere in the help I offered man and in my interest in him and in being at least one friend in a lonely world, I am not of course going to engage upon an impassioned defense of myself or much less engage in violent attacks upon the rather less than sane people who make such senseless (and nebulous) charges.

Dianetics and Scientology are perfectly plain to anyone who studies and uses them. No matter what adventures I have had, Scientology is not unbelievable.

A six year old boy just last night graduated from a Communications Course and was *very* happy about it as life looked so much easier to him now. Anyone who studies the technology finds it helps man communicate, solve his problems, become a more social being, makes it unnecessary for him to continue to excuse his failures with more failures and frees him as a spiritual being.

Man and philosophers have been hoping and trying to do these things all down the ages. Why the charges of villainy when it has at last become possible for any person to follow an easy way to freedom and have a saner, happier civilization?

But then one remembers that philosophers have been given hemlock and that others who tried to help man have been slain in fury and one begins to see that it is a dangerous activity.

Only a being with the highest possible sense of adventure and dedication would ever attempt to solve the riddle of man's being and destiny. The most incredible adventure of all was to advance a solution to that riddle. For the hiding place is strewn with the bones of those who tried in ages past, all far better men than I. So only a chap with nerve enough to walk unarmed amongst savages in far places would ever seek to solve the riddle of existence. That by now is obvious!

To me the only important thing is that I have finished and written my work. Despite all, that I have done.

And man, despite anything he now says or does, may someday be glad that I have lived.

Let that suffice.

It is the only important thing.

I only hope that I have helped.

I have done my job. This no man in truth will ever be able to decry.

How important that job was is for the future, not for me, to decide.

Given all we have presented here reflects a personal philosophic conviction, let us also now present L. Ron Hubbard's "My Philosophy." Dating from the spring of 1965, the work has been rightly described as the definitive LRH statement on his philosophic stance. Although no other explanation is necessary, the following may be of interest: In alluding to injuries suffered through the Second World War, he is referencing wounds sustained in combat on the island of Java and aboard a corvette in the North Atlantic. In noting his abandonment as of 1945, he is citing a sad and all too common fate of returning American soldiers, i.e., the reluctance of families, and wives in particular, to assume the burden of crippled veterans; hence the rash of post-war divorces. Finally, and lest it is not already obvious, all sentiments expressed here were life-long, and he did, indeed, continue "writing and working and teaching so long as I exist."

The subject of philosophy is very ancient. The word means: "The love, study or pursuit of wisdom, or of knowledge of things and their causes, whether theoretical or practical."

All we know of science or of religion comes from philosophy. It lies behind and above all other knowledge we have or use.

For long regarded as a subject reserved for halls of learning and the intellectual, the subject, to a remarkable degree, has been denied the man in the street.

Surrounded by protective coatings of impenetrable scholarliness, philosophy has been reserved to the privileged few.

PHILOSOPHY
RON HUBBARD

The first principle of my own philosophy is that wisdom is meant for anyone who wishes to reach for it. It is the servant of the commoner and king alike and should never be regarded with awe.

Selfish scholars seldom forgive anyone who seeks to break down the walls of mystery and let the people in. Will Durant, the modern American philosopher, was relegated to the scrapheap by his fellow scholars when he wrote a popular book on the subject, *The Outline of Philosophy*. Thus brickbats come the way of any who seek to bring wisdom to the people over the objections of the "inner circle."

The second principle of my own philosophy is that it must be capable of being applied.

Learning locked in mildewed books is of little use to anyone and therefore of no value unless it can be used.

The third principle is that any philosophic knowledge is only valuable if it is true or if it works.

These three principles are so strange to the field of philosophy, that I have given my philosophy a name: SCIENTOLOGY. This means only "knowing how to know."

A philosophy can only be a *route* to knowledge. It cannot be crammed down one's throat. If one has a route, he can then find what is true for him. And that is Scientology.

Know thyself . . . and the truth shall set you free.

Therefore, in Scientology, we are not concerned with individual actions and differences. We are only concerned with how to show man how he can set himself free.

This, of course, is not very popular with those who depend upon the slavery of others for their living or power. But it happens to be the only way I have found that really improves an individual's life.

Suppression and oppression are the basic causes of depression. If you relieve those a person can lift his head, become well, become happy with life.

And though it may be unpopular with the slave master, it is very popular with the people.

Common man likes to be happy and well. He likes to be able to understand things, and he knows his route to freedom lies through knowledge.

Therefore, for fifteen years I have had mankind knocking on my door. It has not mattered where I have lived or how remote, since I first published a book on the subject my life has no longer been my own.

I like to help others and count it as my greatest pleasure in life to see a person free himself of the shadows which darken his days.

These shadows look so thick to him and weigh him down so that when he finds they are shadows and that he can see through them, walk through them and be again in the sun, he is enormously delighted. And I am afraid I am just as delighted as he is.

I have seen much human misery. As a very young man I wandered through Asia and saw the agony and misery of overpopulated and underdeveloped lands. I have seen people uncaring and stepping over dying men in the streets. I have seen children less than rags and bones. And amongst this poverty and degradation I found holy places where wisdom was great, but where it was carefully hidden and given out only as superstition. Later, in Western universities, I saw man obsessed with materiality and with all his cunning; I saw him hide what little wisdom he really had in forbidding halls and make it inaccessible to the common and less favored man. I have been through a terrible war and saw its terror and pain uneased by a single word of decency or humanity.

I have lived no cloistered life and hold in contempt the wise man who has not *lived* and the scholar who will not share.

There have been many wiser men than I, but few have traveled as much road.

I have seen life from the top down and the bottom up. I know how it looks both ways. And I know there is wisdom and that there is hope.

Blinded with injured optic nerves, and lame with physical injuries to hip and back, at the end of World War II, I faced an almost nonexistent future. My service record states: "This officer has no neurotic or psychotic tendencies of any kind whatsoever," but it also states "permanently disabled physically."

And so there came a further blow . . . I was abandoned by family and friends as a supposedly hopeless cripple and a probable burden upon them for the rest of my days. I yet worked my way back to fitness and strength in less than two years, using only what I know and could determine about man and his relationship to the universe. I had no one to help me; what I had to know I had to find out. And it's quite a trick studying when you cannot see.

I became used to being told it was all impossible, that there was no way, no hope. Yet I came to see again and walk again, and I built an entirely new life. It is a happy life, a busy one and I hope a useful one. My only moments of sadness are those which come when bigoted men tell others all is bad and there is no route anywhere, no hope anywhere, nothing but sadness and sameness and desolation, and that every effort to help others is false. I know it is not true.

So my own philosophy is that one should share what wisdom he has, one should help others to help themselves, and one should keep going despite heavy weather for there is always a calm ahead. One should also ignore catcalls from the selfish intellectual who cries: "Don't expose the mystery. Keep it all for ourselves. The people cannot understand."

But as I have never seen wisdom do any good kept to oneself, and as I like to see others happy, and as I find the vast majority of the people can and do understand, I will keep on writing and working and teaching so long as I exist.

For I know no man who has any monopoly upon the wisdom of this universe. It belongs to those who can use it to help themselves and others.

If things were a little better known and understood, we would all lead happier lives.

And there is a way to know them and there is a way to freedom.

The old must give way to the new, falsehood must become exposed by truth, and truth, though fought, always in the end prevails.

EPILOGUE

Since the announcement of philosophic principles discussed in this publication, Scientology has become the fastest growing religious movement on earth. To date, some ten thousand new adherents step onto the Scientology Bridge every week, while hundreds of new Scientology organizations open doors to meet their needs. Scientology has further become this century's most broadly inclusive movement, embracing those from every denomination and every faith, and altogether underscoring L. Ron Hubbard's pronouncement, "wisdom is meant for anyone who wishes to reach for it."

Yet what is ultimately most important here is what lies behind the growth of Scientology. Philosophy, we have stated, is the love of wisdom or pursuit of wisdom, and in that respect Scientology stands in a genuinely ancient tradition. But what Scientology offers, what it represents as a route to freedom—this is wholly new. For suddenly, in this otherwise desolate age, here is a truly workable philosophy that is absolutely relevant to every aspect of our lives and all of it follows from L. Ron Hubbard's crucial declaration:

"We are studying the soul or spirit.
We are studying it as itself.
We are not trying to use this study
to enhance some other study or belief."

My OWN PHILOSOPHY IS THAT ONE SHOULD SHARE WHAT WISDOM HE HAS, ONE SHOULD HELP OTHERS TO HELP THEMSELVES, AND ONE SHOULD KEEP GOING DESPITE HEAVY WEATHER FOR THERE IS ALWAYS A CALM AHEAD.

L. RON HUBBARD